Blogging 40

Blogging

40

Reflections on Telling Stockton's Stories

Kenneth Tompkins
Robert Gregg

South Jersey Culture & History Center
2019

This first print edition published 2019 by the South Jersey Culture & History Center.

Stockton University
101 Vera King Farris Drive, Galloway, New Jersey, 08205

Title: Blogging 40: Reflections on Telling Stockton's Stories

ISBN-13: 978-1-947889-92-7

Originally published as a weblog at
http://stocktonat40.blogspot.com/

Reaching 40
https://intraweb.stockton.edu/eyos/reaching40/stockton_idea.html

Table of Contents

Blogging 40

A Brief Introduction

Reaching 40, a history of Stockton University published in 2011, contains 44 essays written by faculty and staff ranging in date from 1970 to 2010. Written by individuals who were involved in campus-wide issues during those years, the essays mark the young college maturing into a major educational institution on the East coast. They portray lived history in powerful and immediate ways. Published in 2011, it was edited by Rob Gregg—the present Dean of General Studies at Stockton—and Ken Tompkins, Emeritus Professor of Literature and the first Dean of General Studies.

When Rob and I began discussions of what sort of "history" we might assemble, we considered and rejected an overall shaping around calendar times. Such a volume might have started with the passing of a State law calling for the establishment of two new colleges. It would then have moved from date to date until it reached the fortieth anniversary. We also rejected organizing the material around significant events. This might have included starting in the Mayflower Hotel, the first union strike in 1973, and many others.

Instead we chose to shape the volume around the "voices" of faculty and staff and how they saw and responded to the issues confronting the new college. I am delighted that we rejected the time-oriented approach in preference for the personal.

While this discussion took place, I came to the conclusion that there should be a parallel effort to record the *process* of our work. I hadn't seen anything quite like what I had in mind and I came to the conclusion that, in some ways, this set of writing might become co-equal to the essays in the volume.

The result is forty-four essays about what we were thinking, what issues we faced, how we solved them when we could and our thinking about our roles as editors. For example, who was the first person hired at the college? I easily found out reading board of trustee notes that it was Jim Judy, but he had left the college in the late 1970s. Where was he near the time of publication in 2010? Tracing him, I eventually determined that both he and his wife were deceased. Imagine my surprise when I found out that Jim had survived until 2016!

This collection of essays, first published as blog posts, reflect our strategies, plans, memories (frequently wrong), and goals as a parallel effort to our efforts of constructing the *Reaching 40* book itself. While personal most of the time, we believe these are important as they shed light on our thinking and our labors to produce a view of the college's history. We hope you will enjoy reading them.

Ken Tompkins
Rob Gregg

Dis-Remembering

One of the strange aspects of working on this book are the different anecdotes told by different people about the same event. The problem for us, of course, is trying to decide which are true.

For example, I was recently listening to a group of faculty discussing the earliest days of the college. When the state bought the 1600 acres the college sits on, they got many houses and barns—it had been an area of small truck farms and family dwellings—and some of these were new enough to be converted into administrative spaces. My office was in a structure called the Scott House which had been owned by the Scott family when the state bought the land. It was a new house—single story rancher—and was quite usable for academic offices. Each of the academic deans and the VP of Academic Affairs had their offices there.

At the faculty discussion, I heard one faculty swear that the building was used as a "motel" to house visiting candidates for a night or two. Now I worked in the Scott House for fifteen months and can draw—if asked—its exact floorplan. There were no extra rooms where visiting candidates might sleep. Yet this faculty stated that he remembered candidates saying they had stayed there.

Who knows the truth?

We run into this sort of thing on a daily basis. Memories change over 40 years (mine do also!); perhaps I have forgotten that the Scott House was used as a motel. Is there any documentation that would prove which of us has it right? Would it be worth the considerable time it would take to find such documentation—assuming it exists? Probably not.

We both have to keep in mind the following:

The plural of anecdote is not data.

KT

Watching What I Eat

I have avoided examining the college archives because we have been consumed with creating the structure of the book and finding contributors (I'll write on this process later). Once that was well in hand, the next step was to see what might be available in the archives.

Ours are located in the bowels of the library in three small rooms, a nearby hallway, and a more distant stacks area. The folks there are helpful and know where things are in the three spaces they use. How documents, media, and objects are organized, of course, makes them more or less easy to find. Because we have had a series of archivists over the years—each with a slightly different procedure and system for organizing material—it has become somewhat difficult to place new material coming into the archive.

The board of trustee's minutes, thank goodness, are arranged by year and we have a full run from before the college was built to the present. They are invaluable because they record the official policies and decisions of the college. A history of the college, however, can't simply chart those policies and decisions. Such a history needs to contain much, much more.

The question, however, is what sort of documents should be "much more"?

I thought long about where I should start. Should I start with the college *Bulletin* where Programs and courses are listed? Should I start with the board of trustee's minutes? How about starting with the files of the three presidents we have had since the beginning? Should I examine our Union papers or divisional documents? What about photographs and media?

All of these eventually have to be perused; for the first time, however, I decided to read through the earliest volumes of our college student paper—the *ARGO*. We have a complete run beginning in 1971 when we opened in the Mayflower Hotel in Atlantic City.

Looking at the paper was like stepping into Hippydom. "Fros" were everywhere as were moustaches, peace symbols, beads, bell-bottoms and American flags in every conceivable shape and form. One of the first issues in 1972 offers a young woman, tied to a chair with a sign around her neck, and an American flag bandana silencing her speech. Having lived through the 60s and 70s and having been involved in many Washington marches, sit-ins, teach-ins and other forms of protest, it was old territory though I hadn't visited that place since those days.

I realized quickly that what I didn't need was a memory trip; I had to focus on the problem of choice. Which of the articles, interviews, and editorials—if any—were right for telling the history? I was reminded of Jonah Lehrer's *How We Decide*; we can become paralyzed with too many choices.

Choice is the fundamental, driving engine of this text and because we haven't yet been presented with contributions (they arrive in June) we have had few choices to make. Reading the *ARGO* confronted me with a vast array of choices and I found, after two hours, I was happy to leave. The archives are somewhat like a large box of assorted chocolates. Each needs to be nibbled to see what they are but quickly a cloying develops that sends us far away from the box.

I have really got to watch what I eat.

KT

What's In a Name? (Part One)

The current name of the college, The Richard Stockton College of New Jersey, is one that developed over time. Its first incarnation was Stockton State College, but at some point along the way, I believe during Vera King Farris's period as president, it was decided that the term "state" seemed a little déclassé, and that some advantage might come from associating more closely with Richard Stockton. It might then almost seem as if the college had been founded by Richard Stockton himself, giving the college the appearance (even with the absence of any building dating back further than 1971) of being a much older institution than it is.

This move was somewhat ironic, I think, given that the founding president, Bjork, had insisted upon the appellation "state" because he wanted it to be clear that Stockton would not just serve the communities in the southeastern tip of New Jersey, but that it would be trying to draw its students from across New Jersey. This represented Bjork's expansionist vision at the founding, and it was now under Farris being displaced by a somewhat different vision, which suggested that, even while the student body did in fact remain largely southern New Jersey in origin, that it was a college drawing on more select elements of New Jersey.

The college's identification with the region is an interesting topic, one that may become an issue bearing more political freight in the coming years. When the college was founded, the southeastern part of New Jersey was certainly the most depressed region economically, the least populated, and harboring a population that was frequently the victim of stereotypes about "pineys" and the like. The region had very little clout, if any, in the state as a whole, and it was dominated largely by a political machine that didn't necessarily want to see the introduction of a college or university into the area. Atlantic City at the time was a resort city that had seen better days, and the casinos were still not yet adopted as the mechanism for turning around the city's decline. So from Bjork's perspective, while he may have felt that the college would help the area grow, it was certainly not a good move to attach the college too closely to the region through its name.

But, in part owing to the growth of the casino industry and the partial recovery of Atlantic City (though that is an open question whether it can continue), and in part owing to the contributions the college has made to the region in helping it grow in significant ways, the region is now less one that needs to be held at a distance, and more one that might be embraced to help the college grow and sustain its reputation. And with the declining political support for education from the State—such that different colleges and regions may have to fight for the financial support they get—it may be considered necessary to line up support from area politicians. And if these politicians believed that they were coming to the aid of "their" college, as opposed to one that seemed to want to maintain its distance (even in spite of what the college has done for the area and its clear commitment to serve the region), then they might be more willing to do so. So clearly the name of the college itself is one that might be tinkered with in the future, just as it has been in the past.

This is my first discussion of the college's name. I intend to come back to this with another piece on the name Richard Stockton—the debates about who chose it, and why it was chosen instead of other names that might have been selected.

RG

Genesis—and Some Revelations

There is a history to this book. A couple of years ago, I had been talking with Paul Lyons (another of those classic Paul hallway conversations) and during our conversation he mentioned both that he was planning to write a history of Stockton and that the President, Herman Saatkamp, was interested in supporting the project. It seemed to me a worthwhile endeavor, but as a member of one of the younger cohorts (I came to RSC in 1996), I didn't think it likely that I would be heavily involved in it.

That was as much as I knew about the situation until, very sadly, Paul died suddenly at the beginning of 2009. With his death, it seemed to me, the project was no longer likely to move forward as most faculty members are very committed to their own teaching and research agendas, and finding time to pull something like this together is difficult. Interestingly, Paul hadn't been the first person to begin working on this project. Two earlier attempts had been made by Ingie LaFleur, a former dean, and Bill Gilmore-Lehne, a history professor, and both had died suddenly before the project had really taken off. This too might deter someone who was mildly superstitious from wanting to take on this project.

The idea of the project came back into my consciousness when, out of the blue, Herman Saatkamp summoned me to his office. After some friendly banter he got down to business. A book focusing on Stockton needed to be written, he said, and it would be great if it could be done in time to celebrate the 40th anniversary of the college—or at least of teaching at the Pomona campus—in 2011. He believed that I would be able to accomplish this, and he sugarcoated his suggestions in this regard with several compliments about my writing ability and my publication record. He thought it would be a difficult project, but he believed that if I could find someone else to co-edit with me, and if we drew on members of the community for essays and other contributions, that we would be able to accomplish the task.

Internally I groaned, while maintaining a smile on the outside. This would be a big job just trying to cover the history of the college, and that was if we kept it simple. But Herman wanted something more than just a basic history. It should not cover only the early days; it should be a serious volume, with some scholarly and intellectual heft; it should look attractive and be engaging, so that it could also be used for fundraising purposes; it needed to be positive, but not a white wash of real issues and difficult topics; in short, the editors would need to be able to dance on a pin—and all within a fairly tight timeline. No problem.

Herman also suggested names of some potential co-editors, but none of them appealed to me particularly. This wasn't because they weren't worthy people in their own right—they were all people who write well and have a track record of publication. But there were several problems with them in my mind: they were from the same cohort of faculty to which I belonged, and I didn't feel that having someone with similar perspectives to myself, or representing a particular faction of the faculty, would be optimal. How would we be able to solicit the ideas and contributions from the earliest Stockton cohort, the Mayflower faculty? Moreover, as I knew from my time as a co-editor of an encyclopedia, writing monographs wasn't necessarily the best preparation for creating a work of this kind. I needed someone altogether different from the folks being suggested—someone who was able to bring together vast amounts of information, who already knew where bodies and facts were buried, and who was a player in the early days of the college. I also felt that, while I was going to be important to the project, that person should also be the first author of this volume.

I hadn't decided on who that person should be (even though I had a couple of ideas) when I happened to have a meeting with Ken Tompkins about an entirely different matter. Ken started to talk about the early deans and how it was truly unfortunate that they haven't been given full credit for what they accomplished and that it is a great shame (though the language may have been stronger than this) that the history of Stockton and all the histories that had been attempted at the college over the years had never been written. I won't say that I felt like Saul of Tarsus on the road to Damascus, but having Ken as the other co-editor struck me instantly as being an excellent idea. As a faculty member in transition to retirement (so having some time to devote to the work), with a commitment to the topic unmatched by any person on campus, Ken was the obvious choice. Did I think we could work together? It seemed to me that we were sufficiently different enough that there would be an interesting creative tension that could only be productive. Ken will always speak his mind, and while I felt his view of the college was sometimes more pessimistic than my own, I felt we could work together to make this a success.

So I mentioned the topic to him and he responded ex-tremely positively once I had laid out what it was that the president was asking of us. It is still early days yet, but it is safe to say that for me what seemed to be a project almost impos-sible to accomplish, no longer seems quite so insurmountable.

And the material that we are finding and the information that we have been unearthing has been interesting—at times even very amusing.

RG

Box or Agent?

The first problem that we faced when we met to discuss editing the book was what large sections we would have. We felt that if we could get a structure to the project, that structure would help us determine who to ask to contribute. I refer to this as the "box" structure.

We certainly had some general ideas of how we wanted to focus the text. For example, we knew that we wanted a section on teaching which has, from the beginning, been central to Stockton's mission. We also wanted a section on the earliest personalities, earliest pedagogies and the earliest ideas about what the Stockton experience should be like.

We knew we needed to have a section on the future plans of the college; the president has advised us to include a long range planning document that suggests what the institution might be like in 2020.

So we had the time period from when the college opened in Sept of 1971 to 2020. But what might be in the middle?

We could have organized the middle sections around the various divisions (now called Schools). We could have had texts about the School of Arts and Humanities or the School of Professional Studies. This is a fairly common way to organize anything—committees, governance models, union representation, budgets, etc. Include one administrator or one faculty from each School. Initially, we tried this but quickly abandoned it as too restrictive.

As we discussed this initial problem, we began to see that organizing around various large efforts—each of which brought both early and recent faculty together, which created interdisciplinary teaching, which served the wider community, focused on the "greening" of the college and still included our most ancient history and our newest vision, offered a structure that seemed right.

The tentative structure looks like this:

A Different Vision
Primacy of Teaching
Sustaining the Environment
Promoting the Professions
Serving the Community
Envisioning the Future

For us, these do not seem restrictive, but instead they highlight central efforts of the college, allow us to tell our story from 1971 to 2020, and detail individual faculty and administrative efforts to continue the uniqueness on which we were founded.

What, then, about "boxes" and "agents"?

I have a piece of software named *Tinderbox* which I have owned for years and which I have, for the same number of years, attempted to understand. I have had glimpses of its incredible power but have never mastered it. The author of *Tinderbox* is, in my opinion, one of the most creative and insightful software engineers I have ever met. My problem is not with the software but the way that I think.

Let me give a quick example which should link to how we have organized the book.

I learned all through graduate school—and especially when I wrote my dissertation—that the mode was to read and digest copious amounts of research on a narrow topic and then to expand those digests (carefully written on 3 x 5 note cards) into larger texts. This was the way that all of us worked and it certainly worked for me. My dissertation ended up at 306 pages. In other words, the process required that I shape a group of boxes—background, terminology, structure, textual issues, critical history and others—and then fill each of those boxes with huge amounts of text. And *Tinderbox* certainly lets you do just this. Create an outline in Tinderbox and, then, fill in sub-categories of sub-categories of sub-categories until you can't do it anymore.

But the genius of Tinderbox is that allows users to create tiny pieces of code called "agents." These agents then rattle through all of the research data organizing, separating, combining, coloring, moving, re-labelling until all of the data makes sense. In other words, *Tinderbox* encourages a user to have one, really big box. In a sense, they don't have to think about structure when they collect what they are throwing in. Structure comes later when it is needed and clear about what it is looking for.

I try to imagine what our text would look like if we used agents instead of boxes. Throw everything we can find into a file and let the agents sort it out.

KT

That Which We Call Stockton, by Any Other Name, Would Smell as Sweet

This is a second post on the naming of Stockton College.

One of the documents that we have seen, and which we will need to post to the main website, is a page listing names that were proposed for the college at its founding. The list includes names like *Pinelands*, and *Southern New Jersey State*, and many others. Whether or not Richard Stockton is on the sheet, I don't recall now, but this name seemed to make its appearance in a somewhat unique way. In other words, the name may be on the sheet if the document is the complete list of all the suggested names, but once the name of Richard Stockton was conjured up it seemed almost immediately to displace and make the others irrelevant.

On the surface, the name *Richard Stockton* had a lot going for it. It was tied to a historically prominent family in the state of New Jersey, the third person in the family bearing this name being a signer of the Declaration of Independence. That same gentleman had also been important in the history of Princeton (the College of New Jersey), as an alumnus and member of the board of trustees, and as the person largely responsible for bringing John Witherspoon to the United States. The fact that several among the creators of the college in Pomona wished it to be, in effect, a public Princeton or a

Princeton in the pines, with some ideas from that ivy league establishment being carried over to the new college (e.g., collegia and preceptorials), meant that this connection to Princeton would be considered a good thing.

So Stockton held sway and carried the day, but the origin of the name itself is a question. Several people have made claims to be the originators of the suggestion that the college should be called after Stockton. Joan Bjork, the wife of the first president, claims that her husband was out in his yard when the son of a neighbor came over to him and suggested two names of people after whom the college might have been named (who that other person might have been is not recounted). Richard Bjork was taken with the name Stockton immediately, largely for the reasons mentioned, but also because it would give the college an identifier that wasn't tied to the region.

There are at least two other claimants to the position of originator. Many attribute the name to Elizabeth Alton, and at least one other person on the board of trustees at the time seems to have made the claim that they were the key to its adoption. However, it may be that there is a distinction between coming up with the name and being responsible for shepherding it through the selection process. Certainly, any member of the board, along with the president, would have to be given credit for the latter, so all the claims may indeed fit together. One wonders, though, if the story about Bjork's neighbor is true, and why the child's name was not remembered or taken note of; but that will have to remain a mystery.

What was unfortunate in this process, however, was that no one actually took the time to vet Richard Stockton, to see whether he was truly up for the job of having a college named after him. Being a signer of the Declaration was certainly a positive, as was the Princeton connection, but a cursory examination would have turned up some disquieting facts.

Stockton, after all, was the only signer to recant and to later sign an oath of loyalty to King George III. He was also a slave owner who didn't free his slaves, in spite of being the father-in-law of Benjamin Rush, one of the most prominent anti-slavery advocates of the revolutionary era. In the aftermath of the civil rights struggle, and at a time when African American studies was becoming a significant force in the academy, the awareness of this connection to slavery might have been sufficient to condemn Stockton's candidacy.

But since no one inquired about the matter, Stockton's positive credentials remained intact and the college now bears his name. One man who wasn't really considered was another signer, Francis Hopkinson. He was a more well-rounded person compared to the lawyer, Stockton. A veritable renaissance man, a musician and intellectual, Hopkinson perhaps best represented the character of the college that was to be created.

But this was not to be.

RG

Ubi Sunt

I have been saying to colleagues who ask about progress on "the book" that it should have been written 25 years ago. What I mean is that, had it been written in 1996 most of the original faculty and administration still would have been alive and could have added their stories to the effort. They would have made a much better book.

Now, most of the First Cohort of faculty have passed as have most of the administration. Out of the five deans and the first vice-president for academic affairs, only two are left. Of the four presidents we have had since the founding only two are left; the third president died a few months ago.

Trying to find those early founders takes a great deal of time. Let me offer an example.

Actually, the first person hired to start the college—even before the first president—was James Judy. Jim came to Stockton from the Department of Higher Education (it, too, is no longer in Trenton) to assist the first board of trustees and, ultimately, to find and appoint the first president. Jim Judy was the first person I met when I came here to interview; he picked me up at the motel and transported me to the then office of the college. That office, by the way, was in a small strip-mall on Rt. 40 west of Atlantic City, New Jersey. It was next to a pet shop and all through the interview barking dogs and a howling monkey could be heard.

Jim was a pipe-smoking administrator; he was jovial, funny, and had his feet on the ground. He was also a wonderfully effective expediter. I liked him instantly and, while we never became close friends, I think he liked me.

It was natural, then, when we started working on *Reaching 40*, that I would try to find him to ask if he would write something on those early days and to invite him to the celebration at the book's launch. The problem was that no one I could find at Stockton had any idea where he was. I asked the president's staff to see if they could locate him. I asked First Cohort faculty if they had info on his location. I spent quite a few hours online searching for him; having worked on my family's genealogy for years, I knew what sorts of research materials were online and where. I still couldn't locate him.

Then, I happened to write the first president's assistant and asked him if he knew where Jim Judy went when he left the college in the late 1970s. He said he was fairly sure that he had gone to Thiel College in western Pennsylvania. I found their site online but Jim's name was not in their list of faculty and, surprisingly, originally I couldn't find any email addresses of present staff who might remember him. I finally did find an address for an administrator so I wrote her about Jim Judy's whereabouts.

After a few days, I got an answer: he had been an administrator at Thiel but hadn't worked there since the late 1980s. She did have an email address and would forward my message to him. Great! He—or someone in his family—will respond, I thought, and the mystery will be solved. But I heard nothing as a few weeks passed.

It was at this point that I used the "Street View" of Google maps. Thiel College is in Greenville, Pennsylvania, and I had heard from someone that Jim ran a bike shop there called

Judy's Bikes. Indeed, searching on that name I found the shop location and a phone number that, ominously, was not a working number. Carefully manipulating the street view photos on the main street of Greenville I found the exact building where the bike shop had been but it was clearly empty. Another dead end!

That was where the search was left until, by accident, I was in the Graphic Arts office of the college and mentioned that I also had been trying to find contact info for the widow of the first president who I knew lived in the area. A secretary overheard my remark and said: "Oh, she is easy to find. I know her personally and will get her phone number for you." A door opened!

She did get her phone number and also told me that she knew where Jim Judy was as well as another administrator's location I had been searching for. Ah, I thought: Jim is still alive—as is the other administrator—and I can get phone numbers and addresses. I will now be able to write them to ask them to write for the volume and we can celebrate their parts in founding the college. Wonderful!

I did get in touch with the widow of the president, and she said that she had seen the other administrator as recently as last summer and that she was sure he would know where Jim was. I asked her to get whatever information she could and to call me when she had something I could follow-up with.

She called me today. The other administrator was still alive and she gave me his phone number. But, sadly, Jim Judy died in 2002 and his wife died in 2006! What information he could have shared with all of us about the very earliest days of the college before any administrators, staff or faculty had been hired! Lost—totally gone.

This is true for many of those who came here for the opening in 1971. We would have their stories if we had celebrated the college's founding 25 years ago. But we didn't and we don't.

Ubi Sunt.

KT

postscript. I have since learned that Jim Judy actually died in August of 2016 and that his wife died in 2014. I am not sure how so many of us were wrong.

For Absent Friends

I received an email from Ken saying the following:

Rob...

I just had a call from Joan Bjork and she informed me that both Jim Judy and his wife are deceased ... I'm sorry to hear about the Judys; they were kind and considerate colleagues. Jim was the first person I met when I came here to interview.

In response to Ken's email, Herman Saatkamp wrote:

Very sad news. But it emphasizes the need for us to complete our task...

It does indeed! And as Ken has written elsewhere and said around the corridors, this book should have been written a while back. In line with this, we now would then merely be creating a companion volume as part of our task instead of endeavoring to accomplish the whole history.

Be that as it may be, I do think that we need a section in this blog—which I am calling "For Absent Friends"—where we commemorate at length (or even just briefly) some of the people who are no longer with us. Obviously, Jim Judy is one of them, and he is certainly someone about whom I would like to hear more. Paul Lyons, Dave Emmons, and Vera King

Farris have also been in our thoughts recently. But there are many, many others who have added substance and flavor to our institution.

RG

Let Us Now Praise Infamous Stocktonians

I bumped into Bill Lubenow today and he began to inquire about the volume. Ken had asked him to contribute something for the project, and his response was to let us know about a book (Louis Menand's recent *Marketplace of Ideas*) that might be relevant to our project—very helpful, of course, but somewhat cryptic. Would he contribute, or would he not? The note didn't say.

In person, however, Bill indicated that it would be a pleasure to do so, and suggested that he had voluminous journals and diaries, recounting all kinds of activities going on over the years. Surely, he said, we needed to be covering the sex and the drugs, because wasn't that a substantial part of the history?

Bill was joking, of course. No, of course he was! But there is an interesting kernel in here that needs consideration. It may well be true that there are stories to be told in this area. For some part of its existence, Stockton may have been known as a party school; faculty, staff, and students may have, and no doubt did, explore avenues that might not be explored so openly today.

Some of the stories may indeed be less glamorous than we have been led to believe. There is, of course, the story that is often recounted (I believe I heard it at my interview in 1996—indeed Bill may have told me) about the philosophy professor who held his classes in the nude—this being told

34

as if this happened on a weekly basis, out on Lake Fred, and as if it had been tolerated by the college community. In fact, the story is a lot more prosaic than that, and actually led to the firing of the professor—pretty sharpish!

But, it is also important to consider whether or not the things that happened at Stockton were unique to the institution—or whether they occurred everywhere at that time. It was perhaps unique that the college was being founded at a time of experimentation—social, political, and cultural. But was there anything unique in what Bill's fictional journals may have covered? Probably not. And if that is the case, then maybe these things don't warrant a great deal of attention.

I am reminded of James Agee and *Let Us Now Praise Famous Men*. Here was a journalist who wanted in 1941 to cover everything that happened in the lives of poor white sharecroppers in the South. He wanted to go through their drawers and almost check through their underwear. He believed he was endeavoring to recapture their lives and honor them—make them famous in a way. This was not to be Andy Warhol-like celebrity—providing them fifteen minutes of fame—it was rather an attempt to show that what they did on a daily basis was worth noting, and perhaps more so than what Princes, Lords, and Ladies might be doing.

But here's the rub. Even if what we end up describing is something that appears to be unique, by comparison with ourselves and our own practices—the use of out-houses in these rural communities, say, compared to the indoor plumbing of today—and even if these things appear to be very strange and noteworthy—are they really so when we take into consideration that what we deem as abnormal was in fact the taken-for-granted thing of the moment? Was the praise to be located in the private materials inside the closet of the sharecropper, or merely in the mind of the author who wanted to make a statement that middle-class Americans should take greater note of these people and their lives?

In line with the foregoing analysis, therefore, I believe that we should leave Bill's fictional diaries and journals where they are. What they may describe will not necessarily provide insight into what made the college tick, especially when we are writing for an audience of today and not one shaped by the experience of living through the 1960s and 70s.

This isn't an effort to reach for respectability and to avoid what might be deemed offensive for our readers (though this is a consideration). It is rather an effort to understand the boundaries of respectability that may have been in different social locations in the early 1970s from where they lie today.

RG

Searching For Stan Leavitt

After Rob and I realized it would be important to memorialize deceased early members of the faculty and staff, I started compiling a list from the 1971–1973 *Bulletin*. I can't remember all of the faculty who have died though I know many of them; at some point we are going to turn to the present faculty to help us remember. But now I have a list of twenty. So far, so good.

The problem is that of the twenty I can't find the dates of their deaths. I realize that such dates are not needed and that it would be sufficient to remember their names. But, a bit obsessively, I want accurate dates. This comes, I think, from years of genealogical work on my own family where every tiny scrap of information is important—sometimes crucial.

Anyway, I want the dates. I also want their academic rank when they started here and their discipline.

It's the problem of accurate death dates that brings me to Stan Leavitt.

Most readers here will not remember, or never knew, Stan. But I remember him well. For example, he always had time to chat. I could meet him in the hallways and say "Hi" as I did to dozens of others during the day. But "Hi" for Stan meant we should chat for a few minutes. He would stop me and ask about my Navajo daughter or about my courses or what I was reading or what films I might have seen. These questions would lead to similar questions from me; chats with Stan were never one-way.

The other more and more important thing I remember about Stan Leavitt was his Navajo rugs. It seems that Stan had made contact with a group of Navajo weavers and every summer would visit the reservation to buy their rugs. These he would pile in his office where, if you asked, you got to see them. If you found a rug you liked, he would quote a price and let you take the rug even if you didn't have the money then. I bought at least three.

Stan was probably in his late 50s or early 60s when he came to the college; he might have been younger but he was older than I was—in my 40s.

The basic way to find someone who has passed is to look him or her up in the *Social Security Death Index*. That index contains almost 86 million Americans. It provides the date and place of death, the Social Security number, and the issuing state. It is exactly what I needed to find deceased faculty. Type in the first and last names and get a hit. It sounds so easy.

Using Stan's name turns up seven hits using his exact first and last name. But which of the seven is our Stan? There are Stanley Leavitts from Massachusetts, Rhode Island, Maine, New Mexico and Georgia. Three of the seven have birth dates of 1917–1919 which would fit Stan's approximate age when he came to Stockton. The other four range from 1898–1905, which seem too early.

I have, then, three names but without having more in-formation about Stan's life—relatives, where his next job was when he left Stockton, etc. There is no way to tell which of the three is the one I'm looking for.

A middle initial would help as would a birth date, the location of his death or even his SSN. It just so happens that Stanley R. Leavitt is listed under the college's Administrative Studies Program. But, even having his middle initial, I get no hits at all when searching the *Social Security Death Index*.

If I don't limit the search to one database—*Social Security Death Index*—but simply search for the name using all of the hundreds of databases available, I do get a Stanley R. Leavitt living in Santa Fe, New Mexico, in 1993. If that is my old friend, there is no way to tell. If I play loosely with dates it is a possible match. Whether Stan is still living is possible, though doubtful.

One would think that—given all of the databases out there and all of the technology to access them—this task would take a few minutes. I've spent at least three hours on locating Stan and still don't have confirmed evidence. We cannot spend this sort of time on the dozens of names that we will have but for which we have no death date.

I'm reminded of lines from John Donne's *Meditation XVII*:

> All mankind is of one author, and is one volume; when one man dies, one chapter is not torn out of the book, but translated into a better language; and every chapter must be so translated
>
> . . . .
>
> No man is an island,
> Entire of itself,
> Every man is a piece of the continent,
> A part of the main.
> If a clod be washed away by the sea,
> Europe is the less.
> As well as if a promontory were.
> As well as if a manor of thy friend's
> Or of thine own were:
> Any man's death diminishes me,

Because I am involved in mankind,
And therefore never send to know for whom the
bell tolls;
It tolls for thee.

I am lessened by any friend's death; I am even more reduced
when I cannot celebrate that life because I cannot ascertain
his fate.

KT

Remuneration

In the early days of the college, it was easy to get faculty and staff to attend events without mention or thought of payment. The excitement of founding a college seemed sufficient to carry us into any conference, lecture or event. Also, the caliber of some of those events—and of those who spoke at them—was such that most were standing room only. For example, Joseph Campbell led a weekend workshop in 1973 from which we actually had to turn folks away.

But as the years have passed and as faculty have tended to live in distant places like Philadelphia, it is harder to bring them out to college events without paying them. The faculty union's teaching workshops, held each year just prior to the official fall faculty conference, pays faculty $50 to attend. I'm told that a substantial number of faculty leave by noon. That may be a comment on what happens at this event.

All of this is prelude to whether or not contributors to the book will be paid and, if so, how much.

I don't think Rob Gregg and I have spent much time thinking about NOT paying faculty to write for the book. There may have been a moment—at the beginning—when we thought that folks would want to write for the project and to do so for free. That moment didn't last. It was easy to conclude that this sort of work was way beyond faculty responsibility, that a long policy in media and publishing has been to pay for writing, and that if we wanted faculty to take the effort seriously and to produce quality writing some sort of payment was in order. But how much?

To observe that State colleges are in financial difficulty these days is to utter a cliché. Stockton, as part of the New Jersey State College System, has serious financial woes because the State of New Jersey faces terrible financial problems. The sins of the fathers, etc.

A major publication of a large, coffee-table volume cannot be done on the cheap. There are many costs: student researchers, editor stipends, production costs, DVD production costs, design costs, travel/interview costs, copying costs and on and on.

In addition, as a small state college, we do not have a long history of producing books like, say, Rutgers, which has its own university press. We do not have paid staff, contractual links to publishers, in-house designers and all of the other professional members of a university press.

I am not, I hasten to add, complaining. I am exceedingly proud of what we are doing and how far we have moved in just a few months to actually producing the history. I am merely stating the obvious: given the State's financial problems we are not awash in money.

We have looked at our budget and have finally determined what we can afford to pay our contributors; and while not as much as we would like, it is enough that we don't have to be ashamed to offer it. We have over thirty contributors; only one person turned us down. Faculty and staff response has been wonderfully positive and supportive. Like in the early days, challenge faculty and staff and they respond—with or without remuneration.

KT

Connecting the Dots

I had a tiny breakthrough recently on how individual contributions might be organized and how significant each might be as we tell the story of the college.

So far the effort has seemed to be made up of a goodly number of individual documents, pictures, articles and media files. I would read one or listen to one and think: "Yes, I remember that event" or "I remember reading that in the mid-1970s" or "What is the relationship of that account to, say, courses taught in Arts and Humanities?" I hadn't, until recently, seen many connections among a whole set of varied documents.

The breakthrough came with four documents that I have had for some years but hadn't read carefully and fully.

The first is a 1966 State of New Jersey document—intended for the public—in which the State made its case for adding two new colleges to the seven that had served the state for a century. This document is called *A Call to Action* and it was issued by The Citizens Committee for Higher Education in New Jersey.

In this 26-page booklet the Committee makes its case for vast expenditures, political reorganization and an engaged public for what it sees as a "crisis" in New Jersey higher education. As part of its planning, new State colleges were envisioned though not specifically located. The booklet is full of statistical studies such as:

- Percentages of Students In-State and Out-State in 11 States in Fall, 1963
- Hypothetical Distribution of Full-Time Undergraduate Students by Public and Private Institutions In-State and Out-of-State (1965 to 1975)
- Hypothetical Distribution of Daytime Graduate and Professional Students in Public Institutions in New Jersey (1965 to 1975)
- Estimated Costs For Academic Facilities and Annual Operating Expenses for Additional Students in New Jersey Public Colleges and University (1965 to 1975)
- Full-Time College Enrollments in Four States Compared to New Jersey (years 1965 to 1975)
- Planned College Expansion Four States Compared With New Jersey 1965–1975

What this represents is the state of higher education in New Jersey in 1965; a snapshot, if you will, of the rather dire situation in New Jersey and some strong suggestions about what needed to be done.

The second document is more local to Stockton. It is the *Richard Stockton State College Education Policies Committee Planning Seminar (4 28 1970)*. It is unclear from the report exactly what the Education Policies Committee was, who created it, and whether it came from the college or the state. The former seems likely.

The Committee was made up of faculty, administrators and students—all from other institutions. Stockton, itself, had not yet opened; indeed, it had not yet hired any of the deans. I was interviewed in March and came to New Jersey on June of 1970. Faculty were not being interviewed for almost a year.

The document has sections on topics like:

- Academic Majors
- Academic Organization
- Administrative Organization
- Degrees
- Finances
- General/Liberal Studies
- Requirements For Graduation
- Site Acquisition
- Student Life

The connection between the 1965 *Call to Action* and this report from the Educational Policies Committee seems clear. In 1965, the State envisioned in very statistical terms what ought to be happening in higher education in the State. In 1970, the report tells us how far those responsible had gone in realizing that vision. In the first there are numbers; in the second there are majors, degrees and graduations.

The third document is the *Self-Study of 1975*. This, the college's first self-study, explains what we thought we were doing, and provides an analysis of whether we were doing it. By 1975 the college had a couple of thousand students, a faculty of about 100 and a growing administration. We had four buildings and were putting up another four. This document traces how far we had come in five years, what we had mastered, and what still was undone. The college was no longer a dream; it had the reality of faculty, students, classes, dorms, a library and cafeteria.

To complete this thread, we will add a Self-Study from, say, 2000 and, finally, our vision for the future called the *2020 Plan*.

I hadn't seen all of these connections before looking at individual documents. There will be more; decisions taken in 1965 have powerful consequences in 2010. It is powerfully real for me that history is made up of one fact at a time. The whole narrative comes from how we connect the dots.

KT

Ideological Undergarments

When considering the contexts in which Stockton was established, one immediately thinks of the economic, the social, and the political. Many questions come to mind, therefore, like the following: What was the economic situation of Southern New Jersey at the time and was it likely to be able to support a new college? Would the arrival of such a college help the regional economy grow and in what ways? What was the social situation for the population in southern New Jersey like? Was there a large pool of potential students graduating from high schools who would be drawn to the new college? Finally, regarding the political context, did the coming of a college to southern New Jersey represent the growing political influence of the region in the state? Did that region have sufficient political clout to ensure that the new college would get the resources it needed in the future? These are all questions that we should consider and no doubt they will all be attended to in the volume.

However, other questions relating to the context in which a college was founded are those that concern ideology. What ideas did students, faculty, and administrators bring to the college? What were their expectations about the nature of the society, the direction it seemed to be moving in, and their place in that process? What ideas about education were in place at the time that the college was established? How were students, faculty, and administrators viewed? How did they view each other, based upon what assumptions about the appropriate balance of power that should exist among them? Who did/ should education serve? Was it a set of ideas and skills that faculty had mastered and students needed to imbibe? In line with this, was it intended merely to train students for particular vocations, a mechanism for the state to find employees for the positions it needed to have filled—in high schools, in health care, in small and large businesses, etc.? Alternatively, was education a process of expanding the thinking of students, a chance for them to explore a range of opportunities, an extension of their childhood, before the gates of that Weberian "iron cage" clanged shut? Clearly, the former set of questions would be built around a notion of education as very functional and based in current social realities, teaching subservience and usable skills; the latter, by contrast, would be more idealistic in nature, hoping to expand the minds of the students and send them down paths that they might not have even conceived of prior to attending college.

These questions appear to have been on the minds of those who established Richard Stockton College. Different people involved in the attempt to bring a new institution of higher education to South Jersey had different goals. Many of them would have conformed to the more functional vision. If the region was to grow, they may have thought, it would need a college in its midst, both to provide an engine for some of this growth, but also to provide skilled labor for the labor market. One imagines, and it needs to be looked at more closely in order to be substantiated, that the politicians and civic leaders had a pretty clear sense of what a college should be like and how it might fit into the surrounding community. It would be a symbol of growing political power in the southern part of the state, it would contribute to the economy, and it would teach "essential" social values for laborers within the growing labor force. There would not be much desire for a specific kind of liberal education that might be more expansive, and might be more challenging to accommodate in the area (particularly if the values that were imbibed were those of questioning the system, rather than fitting within it).

But if this was the case, then these political and civic leaders did not get what they intended. For it is clear from the documents that remain from the early days that everyone involved was very much filled with a sense of idealism about education and what it should be achieving for the students. Of course, it is important to recognize that idealism didn't come in a single guise, and that once idealism became the coin of the realm, debates about what exactly education should be doing and whom it should serve, and how it should achieve these things, became highly contentious concerns—and to this I hope to return a little later.

It should not really be surprising that idealism would have shaped things. The college was being planned at the end of the 1960s and getting established at the beginning of the 1970s. This was a time period that, historically, we would associate with idealism from the optimism of the Kennedy years, to the civil rights movement and the emerging feminist movement. The fact that some of this idealism was being fueled by the discontent embedded in the growing opposition to the Vietnam War, in the increasing radicalism of the Black Power movement, and in the response to the slowdown in the American economy bringing Johnson's "Great Society" to its knees, doesn't diminish the importance of idealism. Many felt that the importance of educational institutions only grew in light of the growing problems and concerns. Rightly educated, they might have argued, Americans might not follow leaders into wars in Southeast Asia, a place about which they had very little clear knowledge and understanding; they might learn racial tolerance and support the opening up of opportunities for minorities; and, they would have thought reflexively, education would surely help in bringing the American economy out of the doldrums (though this last response would have taken them down a more functionalist track than some might have been comfortable with).

What is interesting, though (at least to me), is the origin of some of this idealism. I will just focus on two examples that I think were important to some of those involved in the establishment of Stockton, before discussing (very briefly) the implications of them for Stockton's early years.

The first is an article first published in the *LA Free Press* in 1967 by Jerry Farber, now a professor of English and Comparative Literature at San Diego State University, but then teaching at California State University. The title, one that sits less comfortably now than it may have done at the time, was "The Student as Nigger." It was then reproduced as the lead essay in Farber's first book, and became widely recognized and extremely influential. The argument was a simple one—that the status of students, particularly those at his own institution, whom Farber described vividly and sympathetically, could be compared to the status of African Americans. There is an obvious logic to the deployment of African Americans as the benchmark for oppression. It is an oft-repeated strategy for bringing about social change, and was paralleled in the expansion of black radicalism to other movements for social change. One is reminded even, of the movie, *The Commitments*, where the main character explains why his friends should commit themselves to playing Soul music. "The Irish," he says (and I paraphrase), "are the blacks of Europe; and the inhabitants of Dublin are the blacks of Ireland." He ends by getting his friends to join him in an incantation of "I'm black and I'm proud." (Interestingly in transferring the text from the page to the movie screen, the director decided to replace the word deployed in Farber's title, which Roddy Doyle had used in the novel, with the word "black"—a reflection of the growing squeamishness with regard to the use of this particular epithet).

The point, though (returning from this digression), is that Farber describes students who are completely disenfranchised and forced to respond to the whims of the faculty, who were the equivalent of masters in a Master-Slave relationship—at its best paternalistic, at its worst fundamentally abusive. The only thing such an educational system could be intended to achieve was submissiveness and, in Farber's view, a robotic quietude ("The Organization Man," to borrow from William H. Whyte). Clearly, for Farber, higher education had nothing idealistic about it, and it needed to be radically transformed so that it became more focused on the needs and concerns of students as sentient beings and as individuals with rights. This view was clearly likely to be influential at this time among students, who were prone to believe that they had been sold a bill of goods by their elders and that they needed to graduate (the Hoffman movie appearing in the same year as Farber's essay) from all the hypocrisy they believed was evident in contemporary American society. It certainly fit with a time of turmoil on campuses, from the bombing at the University of Wisconsin, to the riots and strikes at Columbia and Berkeley (among many other universities), the growth of Students for a Democratic Society (SDS), and finally the shootings at Kent State University.

What is evident from the documents designing the college and its curriculum is that the administrators establishing Stockton were sensitive to the concerns laid out by Farber. Their college would not be one that reestablished a Master-Slave relationship found at many colleges. It would endeavor to empower students. But, if this was the case, who were these students that they were going to empower? Were they really

51

all idealistic radicals waiting to climb the barricades or storm the ramparts of academe, slaves seeking emancipation with an earnest desire to move from back-of-the-big-house to the mansion itself?

One answer to this question can be found in the second document I want to look at here. This document provides a more complex view of these students, but in a way still created an imperative for our founders to establish a college that would think expansively about them and not merely provide vocational training. This document is a pamphlet entitled "The Student in Higher Education," put out (in 1968) by the Committee on the Student in Higher Education, which had been appointed by the Hazen Foundation early in 1966. Joseph F. Kauffman, dean of student affairs at the University of Wisconsin, a college that was witnessing considerable unrest when this document appeared, was chair of the committee and its members included people who were clearly at the forefront of the fields of psychology and education.

Surprisingly, the committee found that far from being idealistic, the students were losing some of this impulse from their ideological make-up. A couple of passages are worth quoting at length:

> The members of the Committee are deeply concerned about the waning of idealism which occurs during the young adult years. We share an impression, backed up by some empirical data, that the seventeen-year-old is a hesitant, vulnerable idealist with a great reservoir of generosity and an almost equally great tangle of fears and insecurities. The cynicism he displays is—initially at least—merely a cover for his fragile hopefulness. He is concerned about the "big picture," the meaning of life, the improvement of the world, and service to man-

kind. He is curious, reasonably open, and eager to learn, to have new experiences, to think great thoughts and dream mighty dreams. As the late teen years become the early twenties, he grows more "realistic," becomes aware of the harsh "necessities" of life, and understands he must "settle down" and "be Practical." His intellectual goals and his service-oriented generosity are slowly stifled by the need to compromise with the requirements of the established order. What was wide open, or at least relatively open, at 17 is firmly closed, in most instances, at 22.

Clearly, the language here is somewhat unsettling, though the pronoun is intended to be gender neutral; but the large majority of students at this time were men, so the fact that this might well have summed up the sensibilities of adolescent boys, rather than the girls, is perhaps not such a concern. The point is, as the document continues to elaborate, that the college years were witnessing a shutdown of the idealist impulse and turning students into practical realists:

This closing off of possibilities and instincts is not caused by the college alone; indeed it probably occurs at a much earlier age among those young people who do not go to college. But the college can and ought to do more to inhibit the closing off process. Currently, there is little in the young person's experience with the college social system that gives him any reason to believe there are alternatives. For this reason, the next major step in higher educational reform must be to look for ways in which the total college experience will preserve for an ever-increasing number of American students their youthful idealism, refined and hardened perhaps, by the fires of realism, but not burned out.

This seems strange, at first glance, to imagine that the generation of "Berkeley in the Sixties" (depicted in the documentary by this name) and Woodstock (1969) would have been students who had burned out. But there is a degree to which the protest of student activists was in alignment with some of the concerns of these educational reformers. Perhaps, the reformers might have suggested, if the students were able to sustain their idealism, their sense of possibilities and the expansiveness of their views of the world, then they would not succumb to the "days of rage" or the "chiliasm" of despair; nor would they manifest so much cynicism and/or withdraw into vocationalism and the pursuit of livelihood and profit.

The need for reform and the possibilities for change were clear for these reformers:

> This clearly is an extraordinarily ambitious goal. It is a vision of social change and reform that is well-calculated to overpower the already hard-pressed administrator and faculty member. But this vision, first seen by American higher education itself, is part of a tradition of idealism which is essential to the genius of American higher education. Moreover, to solve the problems that our complex and dynamic society has generated in the last quarter century will require all the idealism we can muster. The preservation of youthful enthusiasm, which we believe now for the first time is technically possible, may no longer be an option but a necessity, and its decline an unnecessary waste. If this is the case, the argument that such a goal is revolutionary and utopian ceases to be relevant.

This, then, was the ideological context underpinning the work of the founders of Stockton. While many would not have agreed with this need to extend childhood and its idealistic sensibilities further into adulthood, those who were pushing for the establishment of a new state-funded Liberal Arts college in South Jersey seem to have been very much aware of the need to keep this goal in view. But the last sentence from the quote is important to bear in mind, I think. The goal was an idealistic one, it is true, but it was not a revolutionary and utopian idealism that was sought. Indeed, I would hazard to guess that what was being sought here was idealism of the kind embedded in John Dewey's pragmatism. Idealistic pragmatism appears, on the face of it, to be an oxymoron; but there is a degree to which the philosophical pragmatist feels that the idealistic course, the pursuit of a particular goal, rightly conceived, is also the pragmatic one. (And the influence of Dewey is no doubt what the Committee on the Student in Higher Education was reaching for in its reference to "this vision, first seen by American higher education itself," a tradition of idealism that "is essential to the genius of American higher education.")

But in light of this pragmatic core and the desire to not just give voice to student unhappiness, the various different positions taken by the reformers became significant. This was particularly the case as the project itself came to be worked and developed. I will not expand on this right now, but will instead end with one thought: At Stockton, all the main players on the campus were imbued with a clear and distinct sense of idealism; the fact that they had been given an opportunity to fashion something unique—a college that they could design themselves, serving goals and a mission that they believed in. One could say this about the president, Richard Bjork, the vice-president, Wes Tilley, the deans, the faculty, and the students. What becomes clear as the college went through its first decade, however, was that the visions of these different players were not always in alignment. Each party felt it had a clear ideological foundation underpinning its actions; but they did not necessarily recognize this in those other parties with which they had to contend.

RG

White Doves Ascending

On Tuesday, March 17, 2010, Ken and I drove down to Cape May to visit Joan Bjork. Joan was the wife of Stockton's first president, Richard Bjork, and so was a witness to many of the events and developments occurring in the early years of the college. She now resides in a beautiful bed and breakfast, the White Dove Inn, which she runs with her daughter.

It was a very pleasant visit. We sat in her dining room and went through pictures and articles that she had kept, and listened to some of the stories that these inspired Joan to recall. At least, I largely listened. Ken and Joan seemed to have a great time reminding each other of many different and sometimes odd (to my ear at least) events that had gone on.

I will give one example. There was an article (which somehow did not make its way back with us in the folder of documents we returned bearing) about Richard Bjork's participation, along with a few of his administrators, in a trip to Camden, New Jersey. The idea of this venture was to leave administrators to their own devices with a couple of dollars in their pocket in an urban center. Apparently this was frequently done also with undergraduate students at the time until, I learned yesterday, an Antioch student was killed and the program was terminated. The intention, I suppose, was to teach survival skills and to have one learn how "the other half" lived, or in some cases just survived from day to day.

Ken, it turned out, was one of the two administrators who joined Dick Bjork on this trip and he had vivid memories of his own experiences, which, had Orwell not already been dead, might have ended up as a sequel to *Down and Out in Paris and London*. He also remembered that the president fared rather better than he and seemed to master the dismal terrain quite capably. While Ken and his partner in grime were sleeping, virtually huddled together on the sidewalk throughout the cold night of October, simply because they hadn't generated enough funds to do anything else, Dick had survived fairly handsomely. He had spent the first night in the warmth of a bus station, went to Manpower the next day and found a day job moving office furniture, and spent the second night at the YMCA. Ken remembered him turning up at one of the meeting points whistling away happily and carrying a bottle of wine. Whether he shared this with his down and out friends wasn't related.

This was a humanizing story, for me. It was matched by a reaction that Joan had to a picture of her and Dick at the first basketball game held in the Stockton gym. "Oh, look how young we were!" she exclaimed. And it is (was?) true, Dick was only 38 when he began as Stockton's president, astonishingly young for a head administrator. But he also seemed to be harboring some of his youthful idealism, and Joan's comments gave one a sense of how much he was trying to accomplish.

Now every person in a position of power, no matter how good, has his or her detractors (and as I said in the previous post, there were competing idealisms vying for notice in the Pomona marshes, and Dick's was only one of them), so it isn't surprising that the first president had some. But what is sometimes lost in the disagreement over the divergent objectives held by contending forces is the intentions, the vision, and sometimes even the humanity of those with whom one disagrees.

For me, at least, our visit to the White Dove Inn provided a very pleasant reminder that President Bjork was certainly a man of great accomplishment and a person with a sense of a vision for Stockton. To what extent he managed to achieve that vision and whether it was the best vision for the college, I am not in a position to say at the moment; but I came away from our meeting feeling very positive about him.

RG

Taking a Stand

In the first post in this blog, "Dis-remembering," Ken talked about how many of the anecdotes we hear about the early days of the college contradict others that are in circulation. There are, for example, many stories about the naming of Lakes Fred and Pam. In other cases, the stories we hear seem to be wishful thinking, and one is left wondering whether they are true.

One such story in this latter category is that of the Candace Falk trial. The basic background to this trial was that Candy Falk, a young professor in General Studies whom Ken had hired, confronted some Army Reserve Recruiters who were coming onto the campus and informed them that they were not welcome. They said that they wouldn't leave unless they were told officially to do so, so Falk went to her office and typed up a letter on official letterhead telling the recruiters to go away. This would have been April of 1971, the first semester on the new campus. Candy Falk was then brought before the campus hearing board on the charge that she had misrepresented herself as speaking on behalf of the college in an official capacity. The trial was held and at the end of it the charges were all dropped. Candy Falk left soon after, went west, and became the editor, perhaps fittingly, of the Emma Goldman papers at Berkeley.

I had heard one story from Ken, that the case had hinged on the use of the male pronoun, that the lawyer hired to defend Falk had said that since the male pronoun was used throughout the college handbook Ms. Falk, a woman, could not be charged with having violated the code. Apparently, when David Kairys, the lawyer, made this pronouncement a great commotion occurred and our friend Bill Lubenow, the chair(man) of the hearing board, had some difficulty restoring order.

My interest in the trial was further piqued on reading a flurry of emails between President Saatkamp, Ken Tompkins, and Candy Falk, in which Candy indicated that one of the key elements of the trial was the action taken by Jim Williams, director of campus security. In Falk's words, Williams had been

> . . . asked to say that the demonstration against the army recruiters was violent (which it certainly wasn't!). He testified, under oath, to David Kairys, who was my lawyer, that he knew that this was false and thus refused to follow orders. This was a turning point in the trial—though it continued to be raucous. Then, during the summer, when no one was around, the campus policeman was fired. I had already moved away . . . and as far as I know, there was no follow-up.

It turns out that Jim Williams went on to a very distinguished career after Stockton, and it is uncertain whether or not his testimony was a reason for his leaving the college.

But getting back to the original point of this post, one wondered on hearing both of these stories whether or not they had grown in their significance over the years. But it turns out that both were very much founded in events in the trial and were both significant in determining its outcome. No "dis-remembering" here—just another colorful moment in the early years of the college.

A report about the trial can be read in the May 18, 1972, issue of the *ARGO*.

RG

Past, Present, Future Perfect

On Thursday, Ken and I had arranged to interview Dave Taylor, the first president of the board of trustees, someone who was a party to all the decisions made during Stockton's early days, from those regarding where the college would be located, what its name should be, who should be its first president, who should be its second, etc. After having met Joan Bjork a couple of days earlier, I was looking forward to this meeting.

What we had planned was a rather pleasant luncheon in the president's office, with Dave Taylor, the president, and ourselves. Ken and I would then take Mr. Taylor into the president's conference room and point a strong electric light at him and begin the interrogation. Well, I jest, of course. Ken had developed some serious questions about how things came to be and who did what, while I, drawing on my many years as a successful softball pitcher (more home runs were hit against me than any other pitcher never to have played the game), came up with some questions that would provide a relaxed tone—things like what are your best memories of Stockton, your proudest achievements, greatest disappointments, etc.? We were going to end the visit with a guided tour around the Campus Center, so that Mr. Taylor would go away having been reminded of the past, and getting a sense, in some way, of where his work had led.

Since Dave Taylor had received our questions in advance, it could not have been the fear of a Reality-TV-style ambush that accounts for his not showing up! Nor, I am sure, was it a concern that the president's repast would not be up to snuff—Chartwells certainly always puts out a good spread for Herman! No, it was merely a scheduling mix-up, one requiring us to reschedule for another day.

No good meal should go to waste, is my motto, and apparently Herman's also, so we decided to discuss the progress of the book over lunch, along with Claudine Keenan, who we thought could substitute for Dave Taylor admirably, and who will also be contributing to the final section of the book that covers the 2020 Vision. It was indeed a pleasant lunch! Ken and I talked about the website, the blog, our meeting with Joan Bjork, Ken's Camden escapades, and many other things, and we all decided, once dessert and coffee settled in, that we should take the tour of the construction site.

This was a good decision. One of the things that assembling material for a book tends to do is focus most of one's attention on the creation of the college and its early years. This is almost inevitable and is appropriate since we need to find all the documents and other material that may not have been archived or may just be plain lost. This is a time-consuming project, but it shouldn't obscure the fact that Stockton's story is not just about the past, it is about the present, and an imagined future also. Given this, our plan to tour this building, which in some ways represents a new direction for the college, would help situate what we are doing in that larger narrative.

So we located some hard hats, Ken reached for his 433 mega pixel camera (I exaggerate, but it's good), and we plodded down into the tombs beneath F-wing, where representatives from the architecture and construction firms greeted us. Immediately after we had exited the tombs, we entered into what will soon become the eating area in the new building. The three things that one noted were the amount of space that was going to be available for dining, the high ceilings, and the light. This is going to be a dramatic space, even including a curved stairway down into the heart of the room that would make even a Hollywood mogul feel proud!

We then made our way upstairs to the Theatre and it was only then that one began to see the simple but beautiful logic of this building. Well, my use of the singular there is rather problematic. This is in many ways four buildings, joined together around a mall-like concourse. As such, it combines all the functionality comprised in each separate building (though function never overwhelms style and design in any of the parts), with all the welcoming dramatic, but tasteful vistas one might see in the best-designed malls.

That might be considered a slight, I suppose, since we academics view the commercial negatively. But if you think about it, the manner in which architects have designed spaces to inspire people to action—i.e., to consume—makes one fully aware of the power of such buildings, rivaling the religious Cathedrals in some ways in their ability to redirect the mind to a desired objective.

So we were now in the theatre. I have seen drawings of how this will look and am already impressed with the building. As a consequence, though, seeing it in the construction stage was nice, but it wasn't such a revelation to me. While it will be a wonderful space, I was not as bowled over by seeing the guts of it, as I was for those sections of the Center that I previously knew nothing about.

We then moved to the other side of the house, the new conference center. This really will be a useful addition to the college. A space that will be able to sit at least 1000 guests very comfortably, along with a large conference room for board of trustees meetings—Dave Taylor would have been impressed with that!

We then found ourselves in the center walkway as we made our way to the other side of the building. Right now this part of the building reminds me of the conversation in the movie, *My Dinner with Andre*, during which Andre Gregory describes to Wally Shawn (better known for his role in the *Princess Bride*) a building in Findhorn, Scotland, where the roof seems to be floating above the rest of the building apparently defying the laws of gravity. I am sure when all the wood paneling is added the roof will have a little more solidity to it; nonetheless, with all the light flooding in, and the fireplace at one end, this will be a wonderful greeting area for anyone arriving at the college for the first time.

Carrying on over to the other wing of the building, one sees all the offices for Admissions, Financial Aid, and the like. There are some nice meeting spaces and the rooms seem generally well organized. On the other side of this wing, one finds the Bookstore, also on the ground floor. This is spacious and should match most college bookstores for convenience and pleasing appearance.

Through the other side of the bookstore one sees an excellent congregating space for students that will house a donut shop, ping-pong and pool tables, among other things. Again, the light and the space are noteworthy, as is the other fireplace around which our students will gather in the winter.

Heading upstairs one finds more offices associated with the one-stop approach to Student Affairs, things like advising, as well as considerable space laid out for student clubs. Here too is the new space devoted to WLFR and SSTV, which I quickly laid claim to, setting up the ARHU banner, before anyone else could attempt to grab it.

That's about it. The Campus Center will be an impressive building. While it is going to be very busy inside, so much so that one wonders what traffic will remain on the old spine of

A through N, it will nonetheless feel spacious, with light and exquisite vistas throughout. I am, I have to confess, far more positive about the "Old Spine" architecturally than many others, but I too believe that when this new edifice is completed it will have added significantly to the college and to the pleasure of studying and working here, making our college altogether a more appealing place to attend and visit.

So, in one day, and in one entry, we were able to deal in the past, present, and future perfect tenses.

RG

Beached!

I recently saw the movie *Into the Storm* about the war years of Winston Churchill—1940 to 1945. The film apparently accurately portrays Churchill's accomplishments and the gigantic ego that produced them.

It is framed by a visit to the French seaside in 1945 after the end of the war. Churchill is waiting for the results of an election, which, when the results are known, will cast him out of power. In 1945, he seems like a troglodyte arguing a set of values that are no longer needed or important. He was—as we say today—"out of touch."

He is also a tragic figure washed up like so many Amtracs on the beaches of Normandy.

Coincidently, I have been spending a good deal of my thinking time reviewing my tenure as the first Dean of General Studies. I have to write a fairly long piece for the book and have been mentally noting various events in the five years that I held that office.

The movie was the penny dropped in my thoughts about the years 1970 to 1971. I am not, of course, in any way comparing myself to Churchill except in one small sense—those who have one set of skills for an imperative task frequently don't seem to have the requisite skills to survive it.

I think that I did have some of the skills necessary to start a college. I am fairly imaginative, generally flexible, not a particularly good team player, an indefatigable worker, love change, am not particularly or rigidly ideological and strive for the goal rather than the process. I am also not afraid to fail. At least, this is how I see myself.

Whether this set of skills is the set needed for starting up an institution others will have to judge; from my perspective, these are what made me functional for five years.

Interestingly enough, all of the original deans and the first VP of Academic Affairs were, for a variety of reasons, gone after five years. It's as if we had created the college and, a bit like salmon, could not survive in the institution we had created.

I began to get intimations that my role was no longer important when at a meeting of the deans and college planners, we spent at least a half-hour discussing the color of the lamps and lampshades for faculty offices! Something had happened along the way that I—and I assume the other deans—had not seen happening. We were no longer discussing issues of pedagogy, curricular design, academic structure and the hiring of faculty. Instead we had unknowingly become administrators forced to deal with daily issues of who gets what in their offices.

The shift was subtle—so subtle that we didn't see it coming—and then we were out of touch. The college legitimately needed deans who could handle budgets (I couldn't), who could work for short-term goals (What will the college calendar look like for the next term?),

The founding deans (top to bottom): Phil Klukoff (ARHU), Dan Moury (NAMS), John Rickert (BSNS), Woody Thrombley (SOBL); Ken Tompkins (GENS).

and who were prepared to enforce the policies that the founding deans had thought up (I was going to have problems with this one also).

All of this reminds me of Tennyson's *Ulysses*. In that great poem after a perilous decade trying to return home, Ulysses can't stand the drudgery of everyday ruling in Ithaca. So, he decides to set forth again for one last voyage. He leaves his son, Telemachus, to rule in his stead. Telemachus is good, solid, capable and dutiful. Ulysses is none of these. One is not better than the other is; they simply serve in different ways.

> This is my son, mine own Telemachus,
> To whom I leave the sceptre and the isle—
> Well-loved of me, discerning to fulfil
> This labour, by slow prudence to make mild
> A rugged people, and through soft degrees
> Subdue them to the useful and the good.
> Most blameless is he, centred in the sphere
> Of common duties, decent not to fail
> In offices of tenderness, and pay
> Meet adoration to my household gods,
> When I am gone. He works his work, I mine.

The founding deans generally, did not have the skills or the interest in discussing lampshades—not after the daily excitement of actually starting a college. For fifteen months we imagined what Stockton might be like in 2010. Those were heady times.

But, finally, each of us had been beached after the struggle. We could not become the person left behind; so, each of us set out on a new voyage. *He works his work, I mine.*

KT

What Have We Done?

Yesterday was a day for considering the history of the college once again, but also for learning more about one of the initiatives of the last twenty years that has had a great impact on the college and its reputation in New Jersey.

Our meeting with Dave Taylor, the first chair of the Stockton College board of trustees, occurred today, and it was a wonderful occasion. Dave came to the college with his wife, Beni, and Ken and I joined them and the president for a very pleasant lunch. This was a great deal of fun, and Dave Taylor had an excellent memory for all the events that occurred so long ago. Ken had sent Herman a picture of the ground-breaking ceremony, which he had added as his office computer's screen saver. It pictured Dave sitting alongside other members of the platform party, while Hap Farley, then the State Senator representing Southern New Jersey (who had been a strong advocate of bringing the college to the region), was speaking. Dave laughed about Hap and indicated that he had to persuade the Senator to do a number of things and it was always a tough call for him to make—the Haphazard of being the chair of the board at the time, I injected to a general groan of displeasure!

Many other things were learned during lunch, which I think Ken will have honed in on, during his interview with Dave, later in the day (the audio of this has been uploaded to the volume web site).

The president also recounted one story that Elizabeth Alton had recounted in her book on the early years at Stockton. Apparently, when she observed all the students and faculty entering the Mayflower Hotel for the beginning of the first term, some of them a little more ragged and hippy-ish than would have been to her taste, she thought to herself, "My goodness, what have we done?"

After lunch, we decided that although we should take Dave around the Campus Center, Beni would not be up to clamoring through the construction site. So we took her to the balcony at the end of F-wing to view the building, and then we all accompanied her to look at the new extension to the Holocaust Resource Center in the library. She and I then remained there to talk with Gail Rosenthal, Director of the Center, while Herman, Dave, and Ken wondered off to inspect the progress of the construction.

I cannot comment on the trip around the Campus Center, but you can read about the building in a previous entry. I can report, however, that Dave Taylor seemed bowled over by the growth of the college and all that had been created since he left the board after twelve years of service in 1981. I believe that he felt that his work had reaped great benefits for South Jersey, and that were he to comment in the vein of Elizabeth Alton it would have been a more positive exclamation: "My goodness, look what has been achieved!"

But Beni Taylor and I were to learn of another couple of uses for this phrase. We listened to Gail recount the origin of the Resource Center and all the work that has occurred there, particularly the work focusing on the many survivors from the Holocaust in the South Jersey region.

We also watched a 10-minute NBC supported documentary called, "Rails of the Holocaust: A Journey to Stockton College." This documentary covered the recent expansion of the Center, the creation of a sculpture at the new entrance, and the endeavor to secure some rails from Poland—rails that had been used to carry the cattle-cars that had transported so many of the victims of the Holocaust to Auschwitz, where most of them would be exterminated at the hands of the Nazis.

The great accomplishment in the establishment of this architectural memorial to the Holocaust could easily inspire the positive exclamation, "Look what we have achieved!" Stockton, after all, has been in the forefront of educating residents of New Jersey about the horrors of the Holocaust and the ever-present and continuing danger of genocidal outbreaks occurring around the world.

Of course, what this Resource Center memorializes can only inspire a negative exhortation about human history—"What have we done?" indeed! But as Dave and Beni wandered back down the corridor of the college they had helped to create, the more positive meaning for the phrase came back to the fore, and an overall feeling of purpose and accomplishment prevailed.

RG

Forks and Cedars

Rob posted a picture of the groundbreaking ceremony for the college; the event took place on Dec 9, 1970. In a follow-up article written on December 10, 1970, it was noted that a cedar tree that had been saved from the bulldozer had been planted to commemorate the event.

In looking at the picture, I can see to the right horizon a tiny sliver of the main lake we have on campus so the lake was on the left of the platform party.

I note this here because for forty years I have maintained that the groundbreaking ceremony was held quite a distance away from the lake; there is, however, no way that the photograph "works" at the site that I have been advocating for four decades. So, I am determined to find the actual site or someplace near where the site—because of the view of the lake—would have to have been shot from.

There is a wide grassy area near the end of the lake that is a likely candidate. It is just outside of the original buildings and would have been a natural spot for the groundbreaking. The problem is where on the grassy area would the platform have stood?

In back of the platform there is an oak tree that has a fork partly up the trunk so I thought I would look for a forked oak near the grassy area. Most of the oak trees near the area are either (1) too young or (2) don't have a fork. One, however, does; it is large and exactly in the place one would expect given the geography of the black and white photo.

Photo of Groundbreaking, December 9, 1970. Below is photo of oak tree with fork (approximately halfway between the Arts & Science building and the lit path of Lake Fred.

This suggests, at least to me, that the area below this tree is where the platform stood. All of the details in the original photo sufficiently match this site to make it very likely that here is where the groundbreaking ceremony took place. Oh, yes. This site is about 50 feet from the corner of one of the original buildings.

But what about the tree planted at the same time? Here is the *Philadelphia Evening Bulletin* article describing it.

> Dr. Richard E. Bjork, college president, turned over the first spadeful of soil. He then broke tradition by following the groundbreaking by taking part in a tree-planting.
>
> He said the young cedar was "snatched from the jaws of a ground-clearing bulldozer" and symbolized the institution's concern with ecology and the environment.

So, 40 years later, where is this cedar snatched from the jaws of a bulldozer?

The exact site is, today, unknown though I have a strong guess. First, it would not have been far from the groundbreaking ceremony site—no one is going to walk far on a December day to watch a tree be planted. Exactly opposite from where the platform probably was is a single cedar on a grassy plot. It is a dozen feet from a nearby stand of oaks and pines. I'm convinced this is the same tree planted after the groundbreaking ceremony.

I think, then, that we can fairly safely claim that we know about where the groundbreaking ceremony was held and where the cedar they planted is. I sure hope the college permanently marks both so that 40 years from now someone isn't going to have to repeat my work. We move forward in small steps.

KT

AWP

Rob and I have begun to notice that there are some documents that are more primary, more basic, more foundational than others (this is true of pictures as well; for example, the groundbreaking picture is certainly more important, more absolute, more fundamental than, say, Pres. Bjork at Stockton's very first basketball game).

We have mentioned before that there is a sequence of documents beginning with the 1965 *Call to Action*, the 1970 *Educational Policies Committee Report* and the 1974 *Self-Study Report* that form a basis for viewing the college as it was formed.

However, there is one set of documents that seem to precede all others in terms of pedagogical vision. That is a set of 30+ titles officially called the *Academic Working Papers*—colloquially referred to as *AWP*. Rob and I have named these as "foundational documents" in that there aren't any below them in significance and influence.

When the deans arrived on July 1, 1970, a few of the *AWP*s were written or in outline form. Our task was to revise and flesh out these documents as we discussed them and the ideas they represented. For example, as the first Dean of General Studies, I saw that there were two *AWP*s that dealt with my division: (1) *AWP2* which was titled "General and Liberal Studies" and (2) *AWP9* which was a description of the Division of General Studies. Neither had been written until my division—like all of the other divisions—became part of the debate about the structure of the college; I wrote the first version as a result of these wide-ranging discussions. I then shared it with the other deans and the discussion started again. It took us most of the summer of 1970 to write the 30 original *AWP*s.

There is, however, no doubt but that the most important of these documents was *AWP*1 entitled simply "General Principles." It was written on Dec 26, 1970, by the first Academic VP, Wes Tilley. It reflects the long and sometimes difficult discussions of all of us during the summer of 1970. Tilley could have written it before we arrived and it would have dominated and shaped the subsequent discussion. Instead, he waited until the discussion was almost finished and then produced a document that summarized our best and most innovative thinking.

The "We" of *AWP*1 carries serious weight because the ideas it contains really were OUR ideas. This gave the document an importance and validity that it wouldn't have had Tilley established the general principles before we arrived.

Fundamentally, we argue that the heartbeat of a college is dialogue and that the better and wider the dialogue, the better the education. The concept that all voices have importance and must be heard is central to the dialogue we envisioned.

Dialogue, however, demands facts, proofs, questions, answers and principles; perforce, then, dialogue accompanies and follows learning.

*AWP*1 reveals the fact that the founding deans were uncomfortable (some of us were downright aggressive in our opposition) to traditional barriers or walls or boundaries of colleges, departments, disciplines and services generally offered at mainstream institutions. We wanted to shatter those limitations. *AWP*1 mentions erasing the traditional, definitional lines between the classroom and extra-curricular activities. We tried very hard to think about a college where there wasn't classroom life and outside-the-classroom life. Once again, all things fed into the dialogue and flowed back into all things from the dialogue.

Perhaps one of the most innovative ideas is Principle 6. It suggests that all things at the college—including the buildings and facilities—come out of the college's educational objectives. This, it claimed, was the opposite of what most educational institutions did. We hope to have an essay in the book about this.

Clearly, one of our early concerns was whether students could make informed choices about their curriculum. This was particularly true in General Studies. I had decided early on that there should be no restrictions in the GS curriculum and that students should follow their interests if the courses were offered. The counter argument—mostly from First Cohort faculty—was that we would, say, be graduating students who never had a math course or a history course or an accounting course. Exactly! Actually, when you think about it, American colleges graduate students all the time are ignorant of wide areas of the college's offerings. I prevailed for a year or so but eventually the faculty—under a new Dean of General Studies—voted in restrictions. Students were required to have two arts & humanities courses, two science courses, two social science courses, etc.

Such requirements are what the "educational establishment" prefers—they provide work for graduate students and young faculty—and we insisted on breaking the power of that establishment whenever we could.

The other issue that played a part in whether students could make such choices was our rejection of the *in loco parentis* concept. Other institutions saw themselves as standing in the place of parents; rules—and there were lots of them—were formulated AS IF the college was parental. The culture of the new colleges started in the late 1960–1970 period rejected this practice universally and Stockton was no exception. There were all sorts of support services in traditional schools that we had no intentions of creating at Stockton (actually, years later, we did create them but that is another story).

President Bjork was a strong advocate of NOT being *in loco parentis*. He argued against such services as psychological counseling and health services.

These proposals were radical in 1970; from the long historic perspective of today though, they are not very shocking or different. Applying these ideas at the beginning, however, was a very different thing.

KT

(To be cont'd)

A Little Help From My Friends

Dan Moury visited the college last week; it was the second time he had returned since he left in 1975. Dan was the first Dean of the Natural Sciences and Mathematics Division (NAMS) and is the other surviving founding dean.

Dan and I came to work at the college on July 1, 1970; we were both interviewed and hired in March of that year. As I said, he and I are the only surviving deans from a large group of the first administrative staff.

It was writing for the Book that brought Dan back. When I initially found him—on Facebook, of all places—he admitted that he hadn't thought much about Stockton since he had left but was delighted to reminisce about his days here, his faculty and his innovative designs for science labs.

He was here for four days meeting friends, former faculty, Rob and me and the president. You could see the delight he experienced as the past became real again from chatting about his life then and since. For example, I sat in on his meeting with the president, and someone who didn't know either might think that they were old friends. The conversation went something like this:

> Dan: In the 1980s I was VP of Academic Affairs at X college.
>
> President Saatkamp: Did you know Joe Smith who was the president at X college.

Dan: Yes, I had known Joe for many years having met him when he ran X Foundation.

President Saatkamp: Yes, that was where I met him.
Dan: After that, I moved to Y Foundation.

President Saatkamp: Oh, I know the president of that Foundation; it was Bob Green.

Dan: Yes, Bob and I taught together as young chemists at Z college.

Well, you get the picture. They seemed to know everyone in the South who ran a college or a foundation. You'll notice that I couldn't, as they say, "get a word in edgewise."

After leaving Stockton, Dan has—unlike me—taught and administered a number of institutions in the South. He worked at Tusculum and at Pfeiffer and was the head of at least one Southern Association of Colleges. Our paths diverged when he left Stockton; I returned to teaching and he went on to other administrative tasks.

Through all of his life—which has had plenty of serious illnesses—he has maintained a positive outlook and a strong sense of humor.

I wasn't there but, apparently, he had a wonderful five hours with what is left of the First Cohort who were in NAMS. A few of them told me that the evening was frank, sentimental, uplifting and memorable. There has always been a special connection among members of NAMS and it can be traced to a specific decision Dan made in the summer of 1971.

The college provided money to bring in the co-ordinators to organize teaching, courses, schedules and other academic concerns. All of us but Dan did exactly that. We chose a weekend, brought the co-ordinators to the area, paid for motels, meals and transportation. Dan decided, however, to bring his WHOLE faculty to the area for two weeks. They worked daily on academic matters and spent the evenings and weekends playing softball, at picnics, at the beach and other social activities.

The result was that NAMS faculty had a solidarity of purpose, real connections to each other and to the mission of the college, that lasted for decades. No other division was as close as NAMS and, because of this, it avoided conflicts, personality clashes and shifting missions.

That basic decision for all to spend the time together made all the difference.

It seems to me that having left the college until a week ago has made Dan a somewhat larger-than-life memory in the minds and hearts of those who stayed. He wanted to meet up one more time with his faculty and they wanted to renew their affection toward him.

It was good for all of us to meet. Dan was deeply moved by being here. I was equally moved by seeing him again given that only two of us have survived. And his faculty went back over their lives together almost 40 years ago. It doesn't get much better for colleagues and friends.

KT

Tempest at Stockton

I have just finished teaching Shakespeare's *The Tempest* for close to the 50th time—perhaps more. I'm not exactly sure because I have been teaching full-time for 45 years. Trained as a Medievalist, I early on was selected to teach Renaissance literature because "the two time periods are so close" and because I had had a few graduate courses in Renaissance and 17th c. literature.

I'm not at all complaining; teaching Shakespeare has been one of the highlights of my career. Some terms he is easier to teach than Chaucer. As I said, I finished the term—as most everyone does—with *The Tempest*.

Students like to end with this play because the previous play is *King Lear* and they really struggle with that terrifying and difficult play. So *The Tempest* seems to bring us back to the light.

Much has been written about whether or not Shakespeare meant Prospero's island to suggest the New World. Those who support this interpretation refer to William Strachey's account of being shipwrecked in the Bermudas that Shakespeare probably knew about (there is a new book—Hobson Woodward's *A Brave Vessel*—which examines, again, all of the relevant documentation of Strachey's adventure).

I assume that the play could easily portray common Renaissance views about the New World whether Shakespeare knew of Strachey's account or not. Those views saw the New World as a "new Eden" and part of its attraction was that

English citizens could themselves become new by casting off old values and taking on new identities in America. The Virginia Company certainly made that argument though it was frequently couched in economic terms.

One of the most famous sections of the play is the speech by Gonzalo that considers what it might be like to create a new society and what that society might value and reject. Here is the speech:

> GONZALO: Had I plantation of this isle, my lord,—
> ANTONIO: He'ld sow't with nettle-seed.
> SEBASTIAN: Or docks, or mallows.
> GONZ: And were the king on't, what would I do?
> SEBAS: 'Scape being drunk for want of wine.
> GONZ: I' the commonwealth I would by contraries
>   Execute all things; for no kind of traffic
>   Would I admit; no name of magistrate;
>   Letters should not be known; riches, poverty,
>   And use of service, none; contract, succession,
>   Bourn, bound of land, tilth, vineyard, none;
>   No use of metal, corn, or wine, or oil;
>   No occupation; all men idle, all;
>   And women too, but innocent and pure;
>   No sovereignty;—
> SEBAS: Yet he would be king on't.
> ANTON: The latter end of his commonwealth
>   forgets the beginning.
> GONZ: All things in common nature should produce
>   Without sweat or endeavour: treason, felony,
>   Sword, pike, knife, gun, or need of any engine,
>   Would I not have; but nature should bring forth,
>   Of its own kind, all foison, all abundance,
>   To feed my innocent people.

SEBAS: No marrying 'mong his subjects?
ANTON: None, man; all idle: whores and knaves.
GONZ: I would with such perfection govern, sir,
　　To excel the golden age.

Gonzalo argues for a kind of confused—Gonzalo is old and can be excused his rambling—communism reminiscent of More's *Utopia*. "All things in common," "riches, poverty, / And use of service, none; contract, succession, / Bourn, bound of land, tilth, vineyard, none;"— nothing that would mark class or rank.

What is important here—as I read it—is the ironic switch where young men—Antonio and Sebastion—refuse to throw off old, European values (they show only mocking interest in Gonzalo's speech and are at that moment planning the murder of Alonso, the King of Naples in a seizure of power). Stereotypically, one would expect the elderly not to accept such radical change and the youth to eagerly seek it. This is the opposite of what happens in this scene.

What does this have to do with the Book that we are co-editing and, even more importantly, what does this have to do with the early days of Stockton?

Be patient.

I think I have mentioned that Wes Tilley called me in March of 1970 and asked: "Would you like to come to New Jersey and build a college?" That question has haunted me for 40 years. Few of us are asked and fewer still get the opportunity to actually do it. I did.

In a sense, it is the implied question in Gonzalo's opening statement:

"Had I plantation of this isle...."

"If I owned this land this is what I would do" is not logically far from the question Wes Tilley asked me. The thing that strikes me over and over is not the creation of the college but how quickly we made conservative changes and that the effort was primarily (but not exclusively) led by the faculty.

This was brought home to me today when I reviewed a section of a video recording recently produced by the staff of the college of a discussion held in 1995 on the early days of the institution. I was particularly struck by a four-minute segment featuring Bill Gilmore—he taught American history and studied colonial literacy and reading habits—remembering what brought him to the college in 1970. (To see this video, inquire with Special Collections & Archives at Stockton's Bjork Library.)

Gilmore reviews a set of early ideas—General Studies, faculty building book and media collections, interdisciplinary courses, etc.—but what interests him most is the equality of the faculty to each other. He sees this idea as truly radical. He also notes—accurately—that it didn't last.

The connection between Stockton and *The Tempest* seems clear—at least to me. There was much about our early ideas that, to a conservative mind, was chaotic, silly, subversive, dangerous and even, perhaps, immoral. Those of the founding deans who came up with these ideas then found it strange and unexpected that young faculty wanted early to overthrow these ideas with their own (usually more conservative) ideas. Gilmore is right that many things we thought up didn't survive, but not because of executive fiat, senior faculty power grabs, political threats or community pressures. From my perspective, some faculty seemed to want to recreate their graduate experiences ideologically, structurally, politically and culturally. Like Antonio and Sebastion, they carried with them old fears, old patterns and old structures and like in *The Tempest* it was the older founding deans who thought the unthinkable.

KT

To Long Prevail

Sometime in 1987, only a few years after the beginning of her presidency at Stockton, Vera King Farris produced a confidential report for the board of trustees. The report appears to have had two objectives: to record what the president had been accomplishing in her work, and, secondly, to respond to a number of problems arising from an investigation then underway into some financial dealings of the college.

These two halves of the document are very different indeed, and may have been intended originally to be two entirely separate documents. The first, called "Accomplishments at Stockton State College since April 7, 1986," was probably meant to be an annual report to the board. It is comprised of an impressive list of the array of initiatives then under way, many prompted, I would imagine, by the president herself. Taken in isolation this document would suggest a college moving forward in some quite impressive ways.

But, there is that parenthetical subtitle to this section: "(Initiation of Prosecutor's Investigation)," which leaves a disquieting impression. Further, this section of the report ends:

> It would be naïve to conclude that the prosecutor's investigation had no effect on our college, yet it would be wrong to conclude that it impeded or weakened the college and its ability to move forward, to plan, grow and prosper. In fact, the investigation proved to be an effective acid test of the college's management,

strength and vitality. Tested by it, I believe we have stood up quite well, professionally and personally, and will continue to do so.

This seems a somewhat odd statement to me. The acid test metaphor is perhaps understandable given Farris's science background, but it seems very reductive, in the degree to which it reduces the college's functions to the response made to the investigation. One would imagine that the first part of the report, detailing all the accomplishments, would have been a much better test of the vitality of the college.

So this document seems to me to have a tragic feel to it. It seems to be very revealing of Vera King Farris and her presidency. She accomplished many great things and she was in many ways an asset to the college, but her insecurities about her position as president and the degree to which she believed that there were underhanded opponents among the faculty who were out to get her, created a climate of distrust that in the end led in exactly the opposite direction of the one she intended.

The college's "management, strength and vitality" became connected to the strength of her position, and the more she seemed to want to build management, the more she invited opposition to grow.

In the end, the very opposition that she believed was lurking in the wings did seem to materialize. Faculty members who may have opposed different policies of hers, but might have supported others, ended up being implacably opposed to her. Distrust of the administration grew to unfortunate levels, and some of the residual effects of this are still to be found at the college, though to a diminishing degree.

The second part of the document, then, entitled "Suggestions for Handling the Prosecutor's Report," has an entirely different flavor to it than the first. This was the document that produced the firestorm when it was leaked to the faculty. In some ways it was understandable that she should have produced a document communicating what she felt the board should be doing in response to the investigation, but it was the nature of this response that was a little disturbing.

I don't want to rehash the document except to say that it outlined four different responses that the administration could make to the prosecutor's report. The odd aspect to this, as Ken Tompkins outlined at the time in his own reading of the document, was that President Farris believed the response to the report needed to revolve, not around dealing with the problems arising from the investigation—things like falsified invoices, misuse of the president's discretionary fund, and reimbursement for travel by private organizations—which from this distance at least don't seem of earth-shattering magnitude—instead, they needed to revolve around difficulties at the college with certain oppositional faculty members.

Why a problem of administration needed to be solved by an approach to handling faculty is a mystery, except that President Farris may have believed that the information that reached the press and which led to the investigation may have been leaked by a faculty member; this seems unlikely, as Ken pointed out at the time, and it was probably the case that it was leaked by someone within the administration and only then led to demands among faculty that it be investigated. As such, she may have wanted to avoid a recurrence of such demands, but a more appropriate method of assuring this might have been to clean up the accounting practices in Administration and Finance—which she, no doubt, was already doing.

President Farris outlined four approaches for the administration in response to the report: essentially carry on as if nothing was occurring, which she rejects out of hand; "search and destroy" the mischief makers, which she rather less quickly dismisses as inappropriate; compromise with the adversarial group, which she also believes would be unproductive; and, finally, "develop a long-term strategy and plan for the health and vitality of the college," which she supports.

On the face of it, this would be fine, but for the fact that the long-term strategy is not framed in terms of the initiatives and other accomplishments outlined in the first part of the document, but is rather focused on management of disgruntled faculty. As Ken pointed out, it was a question of divide and rule, classifying faculty into groups and trying to isolate those who were ill-disposed towards the administration, while rewarding those who were supportive. This was clearly problematic at many levels, and the manner in which it was dependent upon a rather severe classificatory system is particularly disconcerting.

The president divided the faculty into those who were always rabidly and irrationally opposed to her, those who supported her, and those who were "skeptical" or ambivalent (though still somewhat suspicious about administration in general). As Ken noted in his reading, "[The president was] seeing each of us [the faculty] as simple, rather single-minded individuals. . . . But," he continued, "clearly, each of us is a complex of opinions and visions. On some issues, I can easily— even eagerly—support the administration. On other issues, I adamantly disagree. On still others, I couldn't care less. Simplification, like the president's, is not only incorrect, it is evidence of a serious flaw."

This seems like an important lesson for any administrator to take note of; one perhaps that can be matched by the corresponding realization (that faculty sometimes miss) that not all members of an administration speak with one voice, even in authoritarian regimes.

The unfortunate consequence of this classificatory system was that it tended to become a self-fulfilling prophesy. Those who were considered opponents were treated in a different fashion to those who were considered supportive, and so their opposition to the president became increasingly intransigent over the years. The result of this was that it seemed that the faculty was left speaking with one voice, with those who may have supported other mediating courses less willing to speak up, while the administration also was left taking its lead from the very top.

This was very unfortunate in the grand scheme of things, both for Vera King Farris's Presidency, which, as I mentioned, did witness many considerable achievements, and for the college, as a climate of distrust grew throughout these years.

Ken ended his own analysis with a powerful paragraph, one that, it seems to me at least, was both very accurate, and, in one aspect at least, wrong. It reads:

> It is distressing to read the President's words in this document. It is even more troublesome to comprehend that she believes them. It is, finally, tragic that she does not understand that her strength lies in her ability to accept genuine differences from all parts of the college. Without that strength she cannot fight off our mutual enemy—ignorance—and without the eager acceptance of those differences she cannot long prevail.

One is left saying, with Ken, if only she had been able to accept those differences; what a college she might then have helped create! But, the real tragedy may be, contra Ken, that where a climate of distrust is created one may still be able to prevail for a significant amount of time. After all, 1987, when this document was created, was only four years after the beginning of her Presidency. She would be the longest serving president, thus far anyway, remaining in office till 2003.

RG

Escape From(m) Freedom

Wes Tilley's "Examination of the Goals of Stockton College" is a curious piece, but one of great magnitude, I believe, to Stockton. Tilley penned the 73-page manifesto in the Summer of 1973, in the immediate aftermath of having been fired by President Bjork from his position as the founding vice-president for academic affairs at the college.

Having learned this fact, one might be forgiven for assuming that it would be a political screed, blaming those below him for any failures and criticizing those above him for unsound judgment. This is far from the case, and while there may be a passive aggressive tone at times, and some sniping going on in the text, most of this is not evident to someone like myself who is unfamiliar with some of the targets. Ken, I believe, would recognize some of those caught in the crosshairs, and having known the man at the time, he would be aware of where Tilley's anger about being removed from his position had carried over into the document.

But from my perspective, as someone who has penned an angry screed or two, this is a very measured piece, a little overbearing sometimes in terms of its language and its resort to theory rather than example to make its case, but very interesting. Tilley was clearly an exceedingly well-informed intellectual who was very self-conscious about what he did, and knew exactly how what he was attempting to achieve at Stockton fit within the American educational landscape. Apparently, his tone in the paper, one in which he defines in great detail every element of the college to see whether it should be considered in one category (e.g., objective) or another (e.g., goal or desideratum), was what he brought to meetings as well. This would have annoyed me to no end, but I am sure I, like the people who worked with him, would have been the better for it.

That said, I want to focus on just one aspect of this document. This fits within the explanation of what Tilley sees as the reasons for the failure of parts of the Stockton experiment. In particular, I want to examine the collegium and preceptorial, both of which were key elements of what Tilley brought to Stockton.

Both of these fit within what Tilley saw as one of the objectives of the college, namely to afford students "a large measure of self-direction" (Tilley draws this from the Prospectus of 1971). They were to be able to create their own courses, and their own curriculum, though the amount of their self-direction (how many courses? How much of the curriculum?) was unspecified. They were to undertake this with their preceptor, who would not merely provide a blueprint for achieving graduation in a particular major as expeditiously as possible, but would rather point students in particular directions based upon deep and philosophical discussion about what they wanted to accomplish.

Through the collegium, preceptorial groupings would come together to create community, and also become the foundation for the college's shared governance—among students, faculty, and administration.

By any measure this was a radical vision, but Tilley is keenly aware of the problems it faced in the educational landscape of the 1970s, and that it would be likely to face for the remainder of the century. He notes that the college had advertised itself as a place where these kinds of institutional arrangements were going to occur in the hopes that it would attract students who yearned for this kind of freedom and faculty who wished to be involved in this kind of close interaction with students in preceptorials. And yet, in neither instance had this occurred. The students didn't really understand what the point of these preceptorials was, and their understanding of freedom was very different from the one implicit in the preceptorial structure; many faculty members, for a variety of reasons, came to dislike the preceptorial approach also.

From the student perspective, freedom was clearly important, but this freedom was to be found at a different level from that of self-direction. There were two, somewhat contradictory, elements to this freedom that Tilley observes. One is that students want to be able to assess whether the faculty are doing their job properly, so that there should be a clear set of objectives in their courses and in their curriculum, and the faculty should help them reach those goals—as quickly (and therefore as cheaply) as possible. The idea of going to a faculty office to shoot the breeze and discuss the larger issues framing the person's educational career, while it may have been the experience of some and welcomed by many, was often alien to the first-generation college student, whose grasp of academic fundamentals was perhaps not as sound as would be desirable for him or her to take advantage of such interactions to the fullest extent. Further, where there was a line outside the door with other students waiting to receive the faculty member's attention, the faculty member may have been less than willing to oblige with such a conversation. The student's freedom in this process came in his or her ability to assess and evaluate whether the faculty member was providing the kind of positive experience that he or she wanted—the birth of student entitlement, which is a far cry from self-direction.

At the same time, freedom also meant the breaking down of traditional educational markers of excellence and achievement—an erosion of standards. This harks back to the idea, then current (mentioned in a previous blog entry), that the student was the "nigger of the world." What was the wisdom that faculty wished to impart, and really, beyond certain clearly defined (and frequently vocational) skills, what right did they have to suggest that something was better than something else, morally, intellectually, spiritually, etc.? This touches on an underlying crisis that Tilley seems to recognize as being in existence at the time, which revolves around the question of what an educational establishment is trying to accomplish? If it is certain vocational skills, that is all well and good—it can be assessed in accordance with the number of people earning particular credentials and their subsequent success in the job market later. But if there is something more than this, and every liberal arts college would suggest that there is, what is that additional element comprised of, and how is it to be measured? In a world where students are going on strike and endeavoring to suggest that their understanding of the world may even be more valuable than that of the professor in his ivory tower, there is a significant problem to be faced—one that comes directly to the fore in the preceptorial.

For if it is true that the student may not be willing to listen, it is also the case that the young professor may be less than willing to speak. The faculty preceptor may have felt, and Tilley believed this to be the case with young faculty, where he or she didn't believe they had established their legitimacy and didn't feel comfortable providing much direction for their students. The average age of the faculty was low, owing to the recruiting practices at the new college, and while these faculty may have been open philosophically to the idea of precepting, they may have felt less than comfortable in the fairly confrontational environment prevailing at that time.

Meanwhile, those who were older and more comfortable in their view of what was good and bad educationally, regarding what their standards were and what students ought and ought not to be doing, were frequently less committed to preceptorials and were more devoted to the more traditional disciplinary structures. The youth of the faculty in NAMS, for example, led to a greater sense of commitment to the preceptorial culture, and closer interactions between faculty and students, compared to the situation in ARHU, where there were several older and more firmly established faculty, who, I believe, disliked the preceptorial approach.

Other reasons could be provided for the failure of precep-torials, but one other aspect worth dwelling on is that, however committed a faculty member may have been to the idea—and there were several who spent hours upon hours working directly with students—this was still uncompensated labor; and this was bound to present problems. If one were to teach three 4-hour courses, and that constituted one's workload, why would one want to kill oneself doing preceptorials in the way they had been designed? After not too long, one would look at the next office and see that the same commitment wasn't being put forth there, and yet that other faculty member was receiving the same level of compensation; one would then most likely adjust one's approach accordingly. Add a union into this mix and the likelihood that the Tilley-inspired preceptorial would survive in any meaningful sense becomes almost non-existent.

The larger philosophical questions remain in place, and these give Tilley's document a tone of disappointment, in my view, rather than one of anger. The administrators, faculty, and students had been given a rare opportunity to create something new; something that would allow faculty to free themselves of some of the traditional strictures then in place in academe; something that would encourage students to challenge themselves in an educational environment freer and less structured than anything else they were likely to encounter at another college. But, instead of embracing these freedoms, Tilley witnessed all of his innovations, and those of his deans, being rejected piecemeal, and really without any true test being undertaken as to whether they would work.

Perhaps, in the end, it came down to another objective of the college that encompassed two different notions that were sometimes mistaken for each other. This objective was that the college should be both innovative and experimental.

For Tilley, the latter, with all its assumptions that one would endeavor to determine whether the experiment was working, was far more preferable than innovation. Innovation was change for its own sake, and something put in place could just as easily be altered in the next wave of innovation.

Tilley wrote:

> During the past few years, especially since 1968, a number of colleges and universities have dedicated themselves to innovation. Experimentation seems less popular, probably because a good many recent innovations have been undertaken not in the spirit of inquiry, which would mean that they were subject to continual re-examination, but as new dogmas, reflecting the conviction of their sponsors that certain things have been done badly and that they, the sponsors, can do them better.

For Tilley, the spirit of inquiry was important and an experiment needed to be tested rather than put aside in a rush to a new innovative, and dogmatic, approach.

But, while Tilley might come close to blaming particular people who rejected his offerings, he also provided a sense that he felt that this was really a moment in time when things were possible, and that this would not remain the case. The same forces associated with 1968 that he might have felt doomed his project, also made it possible by, to some degree, fostering the notion that a public liberal arts college modeled on the small private institutions was a worthy experiment. In addition, as a new college, Stockton would have some time to do some experimenting before it needed to answer to powerful forces, a board of trustees, for example, which might not have the same liberal perspective of the college, and the State, which too might have had different intentions for the institution. The simple question—was a self-directed student necessarily what the State wanted in its workforce?—provides a sense of the problem. The question could be answered affirmatively, of course, but most legislators would have a hard time working through an explanation of why this was actually the case. They were far more likely merely to demand the college be more responsive to the demands of the job market, and not simply turn out free thinking individuals.

Tilley's penultimate paragraph is worth quoting at length, as it gives a flavor of his sense of the forces impinging on the Stockton experiment:

> Finally, if the present paper were extended to questions about the selection and ordering of institutional objectives, it would be necessary to consider the very great changes now occurring in American and other societies, and the consequently changing demands on higher education. For example, the decision of Americans to open the advantages of higher education to all or nearly all citizens was made long ago, but

only recently began to create severe problems for the undergraduate curriculum. Now it appears that what a great many students want and need is not academic learning, but vocational training. It seems quite likely that by the end of the twentieth century there will be not more but fewer colleges of the conventional four-year undergraduate kind, and more vocational post-secondary institutions. Yet this development poses a new problem: cut off from the sources of research and study, vocational colleges may well encounter a worse form of the affliction private and state colleges have suffered in the recent past: they will have trouble attracting enthusiastic and capable faculties, and they will find it hard to challenge the more able students as they would be challenged in academically strong institutions. The resulting waste of student abilities, probably intensified by the competition for graduate and professional training, could prove damaging to the society, and would certainly be damaging to the students themselves. It seems, then, that colleges will have to work closely with vocational schools, and probably will do well to work out more flexible patterns of vocationalism, with more varied kinds of academic opportunity available for the greatest number of students. In effect each college would become a university, with component schools ranging from vocational to metaphysical, and students permitted to spend varying length of time in traditional and new kinds of academic study according to their abilities, interests, and needs.

In effect, then, Tilley may have been recognizing that he too might need to propose making the escape from freedom in such a world that he saw emerging. The educational, the social, indeed the American (and later, global) landscapes would be such that those colleges offering the freedoms that he had advocated would become starved for resources because they weren't meeting what were considered to be the needs of students; such freedoms would be considered unaffordable luxuries, when particular credentials were their keys to a better livelihood. The college would need to branch out and take on new kinds of educational endeavor if it were to keep any of the highly valued, but not easily measured, metaphysical elements from simply withering away.

RG

Central Heating

Robert Hutchins—the president of the University of Chicago—once described the modern university as "a series of separate schools and departments held together by a central heating system."

I was reminded of this remark when Peter Mitchell, the second president of Stockton, quoted it in an interview just before he left Stockton to take up a position in Massachusetts.

The remark summarizes a fact about American higher education: not much connects departments in colleges and universities. Many, of course, give lip-service to how wonderfully linked they are, but the truth is that there is very little holding them together.

When the deans first began to think about how the college might be organized, it was a revelation that all of us had had bad experiences in traditional departments. For example, we found them restrictive, fiercely competitive, wasteful, frequently divided into factions and dominated by senior faculty or, more likely, a martinet of a chairman.

We saw traditional departments and power-grabbing chairmen as having the most severe, unhealthy and debilitating power over junior faculty and we wanted no part of that traditional arrangement.

I think, among the deans, I was the only one who had been a chairman so we tended not to see the academic world from that perspective. Having been chairman at a small midwestern college, I can state that being in that office is no picnic either. I once tried to fire a poorly trained teacher who had been a member of the English department for many years. I had evidence that he was awful in the classroom but he was unassailable because of his long service to the college. I gave him a poor evaluation and informed him that I intended to replace him (he did not have tenure). Immediately, faculty throughout the college strongly defended him. Within a few weeks, the faculty member claimed that I had ruined his marriage and had caused him to seek psychological counseling. The administration of the college rejected my recommendation citing his long service to the college. I have to admit that I had been warned by the academic dean that the college would support him. He returned to the classroom to continue "teaching" and I was denied tenure.

My point is that the early deans—and the Academic VP— did not view departments and chairmen favorably. We all had had bad experiences and were seeking other power arrangements.

The solution that we examined and, ultimately, adopted was to create strong divisional structures with no departments and elected coordinators to organize and serve the programs. Academic Working Paper 7—finalized by November of 1970— summarizes this arrangement. Faculty were assigned to programs (what I have called "a federation of faculty") which are independent of administrative control. Faculty could be—and were—assigned to more than one program. Alan Lacy, for example, was based in the Philosophy Program but was also a member of Environmental Studies, Methods of Inquiry, and Urban Studies. Indeed, most faculty were members of at least one program other than the one they were hired in.

A modest indication of the increasing conservatism of the college is the abandonment of the concept of multiple program memberships.

We are the lesser for the shift.

The central focus, then, of a faculty member's academic life was—and is—the Program. This is a traditional, long-held attachment. The coordinator, however, does not have the two department chairperson's sources of power: hiring/firing and budget. These, originally, were shifted upwards to the dean.

This arrangement is considerably different even today from large university departments. These departments operate without the control or oversight of a dean except in extraordinary circumstances. The department might request a position from a dean and, if granted, they would hire faculty (many times without the dean or vice president for academic affairs ever meeting the candidate), assign courses, and other responsibilities with no further participation of the university administration above the chairperson. If that person proved to be unsatisfactory, the process is reversed but is still contained within the department. At Stockton candidates are seen by the dean of the hiring division, and the Dean of General Studies, and, until recently, by the Academic VP. The process of firing someone at Stockton involves the program, the divisional dean, a college-wide committee and the VP for Academic Affairs.

The administration at Stockton periodically suggests the adoption of the department model but, so far, the faculty has resisted these overtures. Not all coordinators follow the earlier model; some act like chairpersons in large part because their faculty want it that way. Most, however, are without real power and the programs keep them as they were—powerless.

Strangely, programs at Stockton are not much more connected than the quote from Robert Hutchins observes. Multiple program membership offered a means of true interdisciplinary connections but, with its abandonment and without the necessary acculturation of new faculty to the old ways, programs exist in splendid isolation.

We have lost much.

KT

The Road Not Taken, or Reinventing the Wheel

I have taught a course on sports history since the summer of 1986, when I was a graduate at the University of Pennsylvania. My course was fairly unique for its day, not looking at sports in one society, but focusing on them comparatively. Students in my course would learn not just about the history or sociology of baseball in the United States, or football in Britain, but the history of sports around the globe, including many sports with which many American students, at that time at least, were unfamiliar. Since then, rugby, cricket, and soccer have become more mainstream in the United States, and much globalization has occurred, so my course may not seem as much of a stretch to my current students as it once did. But while becoming familiar with more sports, students have become less aware of both their own history and that of other nations and societies.

One aspect of sports history with which they are certainly unfamiliar is what I would term "the road not taken." There is a feeling that what exists is natural and inevitable and the rules of each game and the manner in which they came into being do not require explanation. There is no sense that contestation over the way sports are played and who profits from them is a major part of the story, except with regard perhaps to the policing of the performers, either in terms of their propensity to act in corrupt ways—throwing games for money, or performing no-balls at particular moments to make large sums of money for sports gamblers—or otherwise cheating—by taking body-building drugs, for example.

But one of the things that teaching the history of sports brings immediately to the fore is the fact that each of the sports that developed did so in the way that it did for particular reasons that relate to the social conditions of the time at which it developed into its modern, organized form. Association football (or soccer), for example, was fundamentally shaped by the conflict between the elite amateurs and the working-class professionals of the 1890s, the resolution of which would enable it to spread rapidly throughout much of the world, but would fundamentally limit its ability to compete for many decades in the United States. Rugby would have similar kinds of class divisions that would lead to bifurcation into a working-class sport (League) with heavy policing (refereeing) and numerous stoppages, and a middle-class sport (Union) that would be heavily reliant on notions of gentlemanly behavior and self-restraint that could be free-flowing and loosely policed (at least in the eyes of its advocates). While the Rugby League game could be easily adapted to conditions in the United States, with the creations of downs and the assumption that every action needed some form of intense surveillance to assure conformity to the rules, Rugby Union would only spread initially to those areas where English middle-class communities were vibrant.

Contestation in other areas occurred also. Societies that were divided along racial lines, like the United States and South Africa, witnessed different kinds of development in their sports—the United States instituting segregation within sports, South Africa generally doing so between them (Rugby for Afrikaners, soccer for Africans, Cricket for the English). And gender would also play its part, both in divisions between sports prescribed for women as opposed to those limited to men, and the impact of these developments on fluctuating notions of masculinity and femininity.

Such contestation within sports is similarly reflected in the historiography related to the subject. Historians and writers on sports offered different theories about the relationship between sports and society. The most important intervention, perhaps, was to begin acknowledging that sports were important social phenomena in their own right, not simply confined to leisure hours and diversions from more important occupations like earning a living wage. Two people did more in this area than perhaps any others—Ranjitsinhji an Indian prince and cricketer playing in England in the 1890s who wrote about the significance of cricket in Victorian society, and C. L. R. James a Trinidadian Trotskyist and cricket journalist who wrote *Beyond a Boundary*, the transformative work in sports history. The former contested the notion that sports weren't a significant part of English life, the latter fundamentally altered his own earlier political beliefs that sports, like religion, were just an opiate keeping workers from challenging via revolutionary methods the inequities in the larger society. Without mentioning Gramsci (and before he became vogue in the Anglo-American academy), James provided a description of hegemony forming around important cultural phenomena—preeminent among which were cricket and football.

But, and we will soon get to our point of connection with Stockton College (thankfully, I hear), there were other ways of looking at sports that were less positive or complimentary than those offered up by Ranjitsinhji and James. The three most significant, which came to the fore at the same time that Stockton was being conceived (at the end of the 1960s), were those of neo-Marxism, radical feminism, and black nationalism.

The neo-Marxist moved beyond the Marxist assumption that culture (the superstructure) merely reflected the economic and social conditions of the society (the structure), to look at how the development of the corporation and the profit motive had totally infused the sports world—thus, in effect, making that world a part of the fundamental structure of society. So for the neo-Marxist, the rise of media corporations, the growing power of the owners, commissioners, and entities like the National Collegiate Athletics Association (NCAA), symbolized the corruption of sports that otherwise would have been played by people for their own sake and for the joy of participation.

Along parallel lines, the radical feminist argued that sports reflected the patriarchal society in which it was embedded and these organized games simply reaffirmed the dominance of men in society. Radicalizing the notion of the "separate sphere" and assuming gender differences, radical feminists advocated their own sports, which could be built around field hockey and "girls rules" basketball, for example, or could extend to different types of less competitive and testosterone-driven games.

Finally, the black nationalist focused on the racial oppression evident in the way sports were structured, with black athletes, when they were not completely excluded, being under-appreciated and exploited more than their white counterparts from the high schools all the way through the college farm system to the majors. At a time when athletes were producing Black Power salutes on the Olympic podium, many at the college level wanted to challenge the institutional and behavioral manifestations of racism.

Being informed by any of these theories would lead one to the conclusion that to just play the game along the lines defined and controlled by a white, male, or corporate elite, would only mean that one was continuing down a course and implicating oneself in a system that was fundamentally objectionable.

Enter Marty Miller.

Assigned by the Vice President for Academic Affairs to oversee the development of sports at Stockton, Ken Tompkins (Dean of General Studies) had hired Marty Miller and assigned him to develop a proposal. Clearly informed by a radical critique of the role of sports in society, Miller came up with "Life Sports at Stockton: An Alternative." This would be an attempt to chart a completely different path for the development of sports at the college, one that would differ from that found within those enmeshed in the NCAA.

Miller made his sentiments clear right at the outset, "Though the American University has professed [a goal of developing a mind-body synthesis]," he wrote, "too often college athletics has become associated with professionalism, anti-intellectualism, and practices antithetical to a purposeful academic life." Given this situation a new college could take a different, more salutary, course. He continued,

> Stockton State College has an opportunity to enhance the unique principles which govern the general college community, by forming a sports program which complements these basic tenets. Namely, the egalitarian nature of Stockton must be mirrored by athletic endeavors having mass participation by men and women, faculty and administration and having these participants provide internal direction for sports policy. Stockton will not withdraw from sports in an attempt to avoid well-publicized "excesses," but seek excellence in this "art form" in the same manner as traditional academic departments desire a high level of competence. Similarly, the interdisciplinary nature

of academic departments may have its analog in a flexible sports program which relates to other forms of motion and crosses into conventional academic courses. Sports should be a rallying point for social interaction and provide a holistic approach to the learning process which would coincide with Stockton's total community approach. Just as one does not <u>belong</u> solely to a division, the athlete is not circumscribed in a specific role which alienates him from the general student body.

This is a very radical conception, shaped by a neo-Marxist critique of college sports and making overtures to the feminist and nationalist visions (the former here, in terms of "mass participation by men and women," the "holistic approach," and the "art form"; the latter at other points in his proposal).

Miller's vehement opposition to the current state of affairs in sport is most pronounced in his response to the Intercollegiate Task Force concerning the college's relationship with the NCAA. He espoused a position that was pro-club and anti-NCAA. He writes of the NCAA:

1. I believe that the NCAA leadership has had a racist orientation, or at least has been extremely insensitive to the needs of black athletes. For example, James Decker, Syracuse Athletic Director and NCAA head of all televised sports, is the same man who in 1966 answered charges of racism leveled against one of his coaches by saying, "haven't you ever heard a man use the word 'nigger'"? The leadership has allowed various schools to remain in the NCAA while excluding blacks from participating in team sports—under the rationale of "manifest disobedience" or blatant segre-

gation. (University of Washington is an example of the former case and Alabama, Mississippi, ad infinitum, are examples of the latter).

2. Philosophically the NCAA had a clear mandate in its formative years to combat the growing commercialism in college athletics. Needless to say, the NCAA which funds itself from gate receipts gleaned from the NCAA Basketball Tournament has helped college athletics become a huge industry, with millions made at various games.

After further analysis of the NCAA, in which he suggests that joining it would limit the possibilities for Stockton students, he concludes: "Thus, the NCAA framework does not seem compatible with the goals of having sport open to the general student population, and for the most proficient athletes to develop their skills to the maximum."

In another document, the outline of a "Proposed Supporting Program in Life Sports," Miller proceeds to expand further on what he sees as a more ideal relationship between sports and the academy. He writes:

Throughout traditional academic history, a professed goal of the college curriculum has been the study of man in his entirety; a synthesis of mind and body, spirit and matter, which encompasses the multi-faceted human experience. Sport, that broad area of movement, evolving from games, ritual, drama, and the arts, has been relegated to a rather subordinate and very often meaningless role in understanding man's interaction with the structures of society. On one hand, a burgeoning interest in spectator sports has generated separate professional and commercial athletic institutions on the periphery of academic life which creates the antithesis of the organic scholarly community. Yet paradoxically, this proliferation of athletic activities has not prompted a concomitant growth in serious academic commitments to study the purpose and effects of sport in modern society. To a large degree, Thinking Man and Athletic Man will remain casualties and reflections of a fragmented and specialized human emerging in a technological era unless sport begins to be integrated into the main body of academic thought.

The analysis here is dialectical. The *thesis* is "games, ritual, drama and the arts"; the *antithesis* is the form of sports found currently in the academy, with the alienation of humans and the fragmentation into Thinking Man and Athletic Man; the *synthesis* will be whatever Miller and Stockton manage to create that will bring these fragmented and alienated elements back together.

From the vantage point of the twenty-first century, Marty Miller's Life Sports proposal seems very utopian, and one's immediate response to reading these documents is along the lines of wondering how he could have imagined his program would have gained a foothold at the college. But using hindsight in this manner is rather unfair. As I noted, his approach was informed by the critical analysis of the time, and it was that same analysis that was leading to significant changes that were occurring and that would take care of some of the more egregious and negative aspects of commercial and college sports.

This was indeed a time of change, perhaps not of revolution, but a time when people believed that things could be altered dramatically. Why couldn't new approaches to sports be formulated along the lines that he described? And, indeed, haven't some of the kinds of sports that Miller would have supported appeared in different guises since that time? While the college would later join the NCAA and have Division III varsity sports (which are far less invidious than is the case for Division I), it is also the case the intramural world of sports at Stockton has been very vibrant.

The sports world itself, while previously highly monopolized around major leagues that were protected by the Supreme Court from conformity with Anti-Trust regulations, now finds that these sports are competing with all kinds of games and pastimes that vie for participants and spectators through cable television and other media. So while Miller was up against a behemoth in the form of the NCAA, such that he was unlikely to have been able to keep the college from resisting its blandishments, he was not merely a deluded utopian by any means.

This is most clear in the fact that he initially received encouragement and even support from those who appointed him. Ken Tompkins was clearly up for any kind of experiment; Wes Tilley, the vice president for academic affairs, and Richard Bjork, the president, also seem to have been intrigued by the ideas he was presenting. In the end, they would not be able to resist the NCAA, but they certainly gave the idea serious consideration. Perhaps the thought of trying to create and administer something totally new and extremely radical— when they were doing so much else besides—was too much for them to take on. But this does not mean that the ideas didn't resonate and make considerable sense to them.

But the sports world is not merely divided into the world of those who have power who control things, and those who are either controlled or who endeavor to create something entirely unique to replace that which they think oppresses them. As both Ranjitsinhji and C. L. R. James knew, the sports world is one that inspires non-participants to participation—it is one that excites the imagination. This is not merely the case of an opiate being given to the masses so that they switch off and tune out; it is rather the case that people get excited enough either to root for a team or to endeavor to advance within the structure that exists (however corrupt one imagines it to be).

One reason the NCAA would have been appealing to college administrators in the early 1970s, in spite of all that it was doing to which many objected, is because inter-collegiate athletics could help to create identification with the college, to bring in revenue and so forth. Sport could be a source of recruitment and the basis for prestige. Such things are enticing, because they do, in the end, excite people.

Of course, what Miller had been suggesting might have ended up exciting many members of the Stockton community as well—and by all accounts he was a very popular faculty member; but the wheel that he was trying to reinvent was going to be very difficult to construct, and when fabricated it would only move a cart slowly along a dusty road. The NCAA's wheels were already so well lubricated by this time that it would not be long before the cart drivers and their passengers looked longingly over at the sports car as it zipped by leaving dollar bills flying around in its wake.

RG

The Train Has Left

There is probably no more cantankerous, anger-producing, intractable problem in the history of the college than the issue of the "tenure quota" beginning in 1972 and lasting for at least a decade.

In many ways, it is the defining issue of that decade, setting the tone of the college community and extending from the faculty to the board to the president to the chancellor.

Ironically, if you ask any of the younger faculty—those that have been appointed in the last ten years or so—about the tenure quota they will all say that they have no idea what is being asked. It simply has disappeared as an issue; most have no idea about the struggle that obsessed us as a college for so long.

If you find an older faculty and ask about the quota, they will tell you that it was a device invented by the first president to make sure the administration had "managerial flexibility." That phrase is almost never heard these days.

I have been going through the relevant documents recently and the history of the tenure quota here is complex and sometimes unclear. It is, however, essential for us to understand how this became a dominant issue, who were the players and what caused it to disappear.

To understand how the tenure quota became such a defining issue we have to understand higher education in New Jersey in the late 1960s.

At that time, the six State colleges were really teacher training schools. They tended to duplicate each other's curricula and, as it finally came to everyone's attention, a high proportion of their faculties had tenure. Over all, in September, 1971, 63% of the faculty across the State had tenure; this rate climbed to 71% in early 1972, but was expected to drop back to 65% in 1972 because new faculty were hired to meet increased enrollment. One State college had a 75% tenured faculty.

The other causal issue was the fact that, by State statute, faculty in New Jersey State colleges were tenured in three years. This may, on the surface, seem an advantage. From the faculty's standpoint, the college has to commit to a young teacher at the end of three years, so the waiting and stress of defending one's teaching and research is over quickly. From the administrator's standpoint, if the faculty member shows no aberrant behavior in that three-year period, the college can make the commitment and move on. It would seem like everyone wins.

This might work for experienced teachers—those at the rank of Associate or Full Professor—who will have a verifiable record. But what about Assistant Professors who have minimum teaching experience? How valid is a judgment made about teaching after three years?

The concatenation of a short probationary period and high proportion of tenured faculty certainly caused State officials to wonder whether a tenure quota might not solve both problems at one blow.

Stockton's founding falls between these issues.

In January 1971, President Richard Bjork wrote *Adminstrative Working Paper IV: Faculty and Staff Evaluation,* a document outlining a Promotion and Tenure Policy for the college. In this document, Bjork lists the various State laws and regulations that defined tenure and the probation period including *Title18a:60, Chapter 271, Public Law 1967* which defined the probationary period as three years. Interestingly, no mention is made of tenure quotas in this state law.

Also, of equal interest, Bjork's document does not mention tenure quotas once. At this point (1971) neither the administration nor the faculty considered tenure quotas worth mentioning. Things were about to change dramatically.

That change came in the form of a report on *Tenure At the State Colleges of New Jersey* (June, 1972) ordered by the then Chancellor of Higher Education, Ralph Dungan. This thirty-four page report covers the tenure situation in the State colleges, what the Department of Higher Education had tried to do about the short probationary period, what other reports had recommended about tenure quotas and, finally, what the report recommended.

Briefly, this report stated that a tenure quota of 60% should be instituted at the State colleges. To insure compliance, each college was to submit an annual report to the Department of Higher Education.

Coincidentally, the AFT was elected as the bargaining agent in February of 1973—not long after Bjork's document on Promotion and Tenure and the DHE report on tenure quotas. These three facts shaped the firestorm that followed.

When the *NY Times* ran an article on October 22, 1972, the bargaining agent was the Association of New Jersey College Faculties, an NJEA affiliate. It attacked the quota plan as being against State law and the US Constitution. It also saw Chancellor Dungan as overruling local boards. Montclair's president resigned over the issue and the reporter states that Stockton's faculty was especially "infuriated."

And so the issue was joined. Four months later the bargaining agent elected—with incredibly strong Stockton support—became the AFT. From that point on the tenure quota was the center issue for the Union because to lose the fight would have meant that the Union could not protect its members and if that had ever happened it would have lost all credibility.

Tenure quotas appeal to administrators in times when education is expanding. If a college isn't hiring many new faculty, quotas are not impressive or needed. But when Stockton doubled its faculty in two years after its founding, quotas made sense to administrators who feared that if the faculty ever achieved 100% tenure, change would have become impossible. At a place like Stockton—which prided itself on constant change—full tenure would have been anathema.

On the other hand, Stockton's faculty was uniquely young in the State system so it saw the quota as a direct attack on being here, teaching, doing research and becoming successful academicians.

Once these lines were drawn there was no turning back to the excitement of the earliest days and to a communality of purpose.

Indeed, Bjork wrote and presented testimony before the New Jersey Assembly Education Committee in November 1976. In his short statement he argues fully against tenure. By then, the issue was already beginning to fade—though it wasn't a dead issue until at least a decade or more—and Bjork's speech is an elegant rear-guard action. As they say: the train had left the station (see Rob's remark about his speech below).

With forty years hindsight, one is forced to wonder if all of the anger, effort, talk, arguing, planning and writing was not wasted. Other issues of power sharing, faculty governance, tight budgets and benefits occupied the Union—and rightfully so. Once the halcyon days of the Founding had passed, the college had to survive in a radically different world from 1971 as the new kid on the block. It had to compete for funds, for faculty, for lines, for students and for the excellence it had so long assumed.

No one talks—or writes—about tenure quotas today; this is true, at least, in my hearing. Concomitantly, no one becomes much excited about any issue either. As I said: the train has left.

KT

Nowhere Man

In December 1974, only a few years after Stockton had opened its doors, a faculty member, Allen Lacy, published an article in *The Chronicle of Higher Education* entitled, "What Happened to Erewhon?" The core of the argument, summarized right below the title, was this: "The new colleges of the 1960s have not realized the utopian goals set by their founders." Early on in the piece, Lacy elaborated on this argument, writing: "To put it bluntly, no new school has succeeded in realizing the ideals stated in the original rhetoric. I am coming to suspect that the fault lies not in the times, but in the ideals themselves, and in the peculiar nature of new colleges as institutions with utopian blueprints."

Almost immediately, the reader is left wondering two things: first, did the founders of these colleges have utopian goals and blueprints, and second, was the brief period between the founding of these colleges and 1974, when Lacy was offering his judgment, sufficient time in which to assess whether or not they had "realized" their goals (utopian or otherwise)?

Perhaps, before dealing with these two questions directly, it is worth taking a moment to outline the argument further. Fortunately, Ken Tompkins has provided me with an excellent synopsis of Lacy's major points that I do not think I could improve upon:

> His argument in the piece seems clear: (1) new colleges will never stand the weight of conservative,

academic culture; (2) new colleges are reverse images of all other institutions; (3) new colleges are not new; (4) educational idealism will get you nowhere; (5) new colleges will let you down—they promise much and deliver little; (6) new colleges offer great possibilities for conflict and for collective disappointment; (7) finally, new colleges offer "unusual chances for academic degradation."

This is a strange mixture of saying that these Utopians haven't been able to achieve any of their goals because of the nature of "the institutional inevitabilities of higher education," and saying that they have been placing us in danger of undermining higher education. While it is not impossible to do both of these things (the two positions are not entirely contradictory), it is difficult to imagine that everything good that was suggested by these Utopians was either not new or unable to change anything, whereas everything bad that they initiated was in danger of causing "degradation."

The long and the short of Lacy's position appears to be that he just did not like the alternatives these "Utopians" had come up with. As he indicated at the end of the essay,

> Were I to help start yet a third new college [he had been a charter member of Kirkland College before coming to Stockton], my advice to the founders would be to forgo excessive claims about the innovational wonders to be achieved, to strive to some extent to be . . . ordinary! I have a growing hunch that in the ordinary—even, to use a word in disrepute at Erewhon, in the *traditional*—there is much good to be found, even for Erewhon.

Erewhon, Erewhon, what is this? Lacy's mention of this name brings us back to the question of Utopianism. Erewhon refers to Samuel Butler's utopian novel by that name, one of many that appeared in the second half of the nineteenth century on both sides of the Atlantic. Utopianism was something that captivated many people's minds at this time. Social theorists, like Butler, Edward Bellamy, William Morris, Charlotte Perkins Gilman, and Ignatius Donnelly, among others, saw the creation of the literary utopia as a device through which they could excoriate their own society and promote change.

Two more negative visions of utopianism should also be noted. The notion of utopianism was often cause for derision—a dismissive charge made by one theorist against another. Left-leaning theorists argued that instead of taking up a critical posture or recognizing that social change and the conflict that created it was on-going, utopians merely endeavored to invert the present and envisioned a static and unchanging world. In the process they ended up promoting their own highly bureaucratized and regimented world. Those on the right averred that, instead of recognizing that all societies were formed around social inequalities that were nigh on impossible to eradicate (and this was undesirable anyway), the utopian put forward dangerous and fanciful notions that only made things worse. One might suggest that the criticisms proffered by Lacy fit with this last view of Utopianism.

So, we ask ourselves whether any of these descriptions fit the founders of these new institutions. Such people were clearly critical of the society and the educational system of their day, as Lacy himself noted:

Anyone on a university campus in the mid-1960s is familiar with the litany of complaint. Education had become a bureaucratized, impersonal process in which students were stapled, mutilated, and destroyed by aloof administrators. The person was reduced to a Social Security number in the campus computer. The lockstep curriculum was outmoded and rigid, the educational analogue of the industrial assembly line. Faculty members were elite grantsmen-researchers, shamefully delegating undergraduate instruction to exploited graduate assistants. Colleges and universities were perverted by involvement in Cold War geopolitics and easy acceptance of shabby domestic corporate practices.

Lacy believed that these new educators were given the opportunity to create Nowhere, and they seized this opportunity to do something completely different from that which was being done elsewhere—and at no point does he indicate these people were in any way incorrect in their assessment of the academic landscape. There clearly was a sense that something new or better could be accomplished, but what is clear from looking at Stockton's early days is that there was never any sense of a unity of vision, right from the outset—a Plan or Blueprint.

The founders seemed to have recognized that they could deviate from the norm and make some changes, but they also immediately recognized that they were working with others who didn't share their vision to the same degree. They also recognized that they were part of a state educational system, that they were located in Southern New Jersey (and so would be working with particular kinds of students and in particular kinds of communities), that the labor market and labor relations would have a say in certain areas, and many other things besides. Given that conflict seems to have appeared in different guises very early on, once the doors of the Mayflower Hotel opened, it seems that to suggest that these founders believed that they would create something that would be moved forward simply by consensus around a unified blueprint or plan, when so much about the political and educational landscape at the time was fraught with tension, seems unfair to them and the projects in which they invested their energies.

The left criticism of Utopianism also doesn't stand up to close scrutiny in terms of the Stockton transcript. Who would the Utopians be? The board of trustees, the president, the vice-president, the deans, the faculty, the students? All of these people had different visions and different goals. They all may have wished to change some of the problems that they saw endemic in academia, but beyond a few ideas that they may have held in common, they do not seem to have been on the same page with regard to the purpose or the method of these things.

Take the Collegium, for example. This was a very strange superstructure molded around the preceptorials, with faculty, staff and administrators making up small communities—almost college-like communities without colleges. But the president, vice-president, the deans, and faculty all seem to have had different ideas about what the collegium should look like, how devoted faculty should be to their collegia, and whether or not it was to have some formal political role to play. Not surprisingly, the collegium didn't last for very long. Some would complain they were given up before they had been fully tested; others would argue that they were never workable and needed to be quickly discarded along with some of the other innovations. This was experimentation not with a view to creating Utopia, but rather, in the vein of a Franklin Roosevelt, with a view to determining what might work better than current practice.

Only the third notion of Utopian seems to fully fit the view of Stockton. But, if any such experimentation and tinkering with the system as it then was, is sufficient to dismiss someone as being Utopian, then it covers almost anyone from the most pragmatic to the most idealistic, and applies to anyone who wanted to see some form of change. It reminds one of the dichotomy that Karl Mannheim draws in *Ideology and Utopia*. The former represents the ideas of that which exists, the status quo; the latter applies to any idea thought up to supplant it. While Mannheim himself (as far as I can remember) was not dismissive of the notion of Utopia, one can see that this kind of duality can very quickly make the notion of change itself suspect, leaving the social being in a position of being forced to accept that which already exists.

As Lacy noted, there are indeed "institutional inevitabilities of higher education," which put constraints on those who would attempt to build something new. But do these inevitabilities necessarily mean that the endeavor to create something new is a waste of time and energy, and simply hubris? Is it a case of the Nowhere Man not knowing what he is missing, and suggesting that he should take his time and not worry, as the world is at his command? Or are there alternatives, which Nowhere men and their gender-inclusive ilk may lead us to yet? My own view is that even after all the limits of the way in which things developed are taken into consideration, it is still evident that things are done differently (and frequently better) at Stockton than at many other colleges and universities (particularly with regard to the areas of complaint noted in the 1960s). This was not the result of a blueprint being created in the first years; it was rather the product of many different people undertaking, in divergent ways, to right some of the wrongs they themselves had experienced. It was certainly worth the effort.

RG

To See What He Would Call Them

Shakespeare had it wrong. Names mean everything: acceptance, financial success, loyalty or rejection, satire, failure and abandonment. A quick search turns up the five or twelve rules for naming a company or organization:

- has to be memorable
- should have a visual element
- has to have a positive connotation
- needs to include a hint about what the company does
- has to be fairly short

Colleges, today, will name anything for a specific contribution. In a *Los Angeles Times* article (November 30, 1999), about the practice of naming objects on a campus, the following list of examples is compiled:

- Your name on an elevator – $50K
- Your name on a scholarship to put a quarterback through school – $350K
- Your name on a street light – $15K
- Your name on a bench – $12K
- Your name on a School – $45M

Naming something like these provides proof of generosity, a kind of immortality, family recognition, and evidence of being on the cultural pecking order.

It should come as no surprise, that the naming of Stockton has become a legendary event. There are, for example, at least three publically told stories about how Stockton got its name.

One First Cohort faculty tells the story of the Stockton board meeting at one of the service areas on the New Jersey Turnpike. Not yet having a name for the college they decided to name it after the person for whom the service area was named—Richard Stockton.

Both Dick Bjork—the first president—and his wife Joan have told the story about having a small boy in their Lawrenceville, New Jersey, neighborhood coming to their house. He had heard that the college was looking for a name and he told the president that he had a couple to suggest. Neither the president nor his wife remembered all of the names; the one they did remember was Richard Stockton State College—thus naming the college after one of the five signers of the Declaration of Independence from New Jersey.

Another First Cohort faculty says that he heard that there had been a disagreement from the beginning of the college as to whether it was going to be a distinctive liberal arts college, which would draw from all over the state, and perhaps beyond, or whether it would be a college that would cater primarily to the needs of South Jersey. Dungan and Bjork favored the former position and some of the trustees, supported by many in the outside community, favored the latter. These trustees were putting pressure on Bjork to name the college in a way that would identify it with South Jersey and so he asked Dungan to preempt that discussion by imposing a name that would not identify the college with South Jersey. Dungan had to do this in a hurry in order to close off the discussion before the next meeting of Stockton's board of trustees. He and the folks at Department of Higher Education grabbed Stockton's name, as a signer of the Declaration of Independence from New

Jersey, to meet the deadline without undertaking a thorough investigation of Richard Stockton's credentials.

The board of trustees had previously requested suggestions from the pubic in the spring of 1969. By August they had received 64 names, which fall into three general categories: places, things and people.

For places there are the expected South Jersey shore areas:

> *Atlantic Highlands College*
> *College By the Sea*
> *Garden State College*
> *New Jersey East College*
> *Ocean Sands State College*
> *Southeast College of New Jersey*

For things there are some unusual suggestions:

> *Berry Bottom Bog State*
> *Blueberry State College*
> *Boardwalk College*
> *College of the Sand*
> *Gull College*
> *Sand Piper State College*
> *Jersey Tomato College*

For people, there are also some strange possibilities:

> *Einstein State College*
> *Farley State College*
> *Pinky's Corner College*
> *Virgil I. Grissom State College*
> *Woodrow Wilson State College*
> *Richard Stockton State College*

Some brief explanation seems warranted. Berry Bottom Bog State or Jersey Tomato College cannot be considered as serious suggestions. Einstein was living in Princeton, New Jersey, at the time, and though Woodrow Wilson was long deceased he, too, was connected to Princeton. Pinky's Corner is a long-running interview show on radio and television in Atlantic City. Farley State would have been named for an incredibly powerful State senator who was instrumental in getting the legislation establishing the college passed in Trenton. Finally, Virgil Grissom—an astronaut—has no connection to New Jersey and is a strange suggestion perhaps based on the fact that his death was in 1967—two years before this list was collected.

The process following the public request for names was this:

> 1. In June 1969 the board of trustees had received 30 names from its public request.
>
> 2. In July 1969 Jim Judy (secretary to the board) reported that 40 names had been received.
>
> 3. In August 1969 there are 64 names included in the board of trustees minutes (see below).
>
> 4. By the September 1969 meeting, the board had received a list of 12 names and the Trustees chose five to vote on.
>
> 5. By October first, 1969 the board of trustees has decided officially on RSSC.

The name RSSC is in the original list of June 1969 so it seems to be a contender early in the process. Given this fact, the question of who came up with the name is perhaps less significant (since the name was offered up early in the process) than why it was that the name progressed from being at the bottom of the major contenders to being picked. This lends credence to the story about Dungan making the decision.

The other question is why none of the other four New Jersey signers of the Declaration—Abraham Clark, John Hart, Francis Hopkinson, and John Witherspoon—were ever contenders as possible names for the college. Each one of these men might have been appropriate for different reasons, bringing something different to the college—Francis Hopkinson, for example, was a musician, composer, and a man of letters; John Witherspoon was president of New Jersey College.

What was clear, however, was that no investigation was undertaken about any of the names offered and certainly not that of Richard Stockton. He, after all, was the one signer who had signed an oath of loyalty to the Crown after he had signed the Declaration of Independence. There were extenuating circumstances for this act (which are contested), nonetheless this might well have given the college founders pause had they known about it. Moreover, the fact that the college was being established in the immediate aftermath of the Civil Rights Movement and at a time of growing awareness about the history of slavery in the United States, would perhaps have led the board to shy away from Stockton, had they known that he had been an unrepentant slave owner.

SUGGESTED NAMES FOR NEW College—ADDENDUM (presented to the board of trustees in August, 1969)

A-1 College
All Wars Memorial College

Atlantic Beautiful College
Atlantic City College
Atlantic Highlands College
Atlantic Lighthouse College
Atlantic–Seaboard College
Barren Pines College
Beach College of South Jersey
Berry Bottom Bog State
Blueberry State College or Blueberry College
New Jersey State Blueberry College
South Jersey Blueberry State
Boardwalk College
Cape Security
Coastal Plain State
College by the Sea
College in the Pines
College of the Sand
Convention City College
Delsanta State College (Delaware and Atlantic)
Eastern College
Edge State College
Edison State College
Einstein State College
Excelsior State College
Farely State College
Garden State Source
Garden State Southern College
Great Egg Harbor Bay College
Gull College
Jersey Tomato College
Jonathan Pitney State College
Leed College
Lenapes State College

Lower Jersey Liberal Arts College
McKee State College
Neptune Shore College
New Air College
New Jersey Bayside State College
New Jersey Colonial College
New Jersey East College
New Jersey Southern College
New Jersey State Bell College
Ocean Sands State College
Ocean State College
Pinky's Corner College
Resort College
Richard Stockton State College
Sand Piper State College
Sandy Harbor State College
Seabreezes College
Seashell College
Sea Spray State College
South Atlantic Delaware College
Southeast College of New Jersey
South Jersey College
South Jersey College By-The-Sea
Southern Pines of Knowledge
Star of the Sea College
Triangle College
Tri-County College
University of South Jersey
Virgil I. Grissom State College
White Cap State College
Woodrow Wilson State College

KT

10 Things Everyone Should Know About the Early College

In my judgment, one of the sad facts about the college is that we have not passed on the early culture or, at least, the best parts of that early culture. Because we haven't done so, faculty joining the college from the mid-1980s until today have had to "invent" a culture and, as might be expected, that culture reflects graduate experience at major universities.

Thus, there is a reason for us early folk—those who came here at the beginning and into the 1970s—to sense that we are more like those major universities each day.

Let me hasten to add that some of the ideas we had when the college opened were not good ones. Perhaps the best example was the idea that we would not have a remedial writing program here; instead, each faculty would teach writing in the context of their courses. In a sense we would not have a "writing problem" because all of us had a writing problem and we would deal with it individually.

All of this made sense in the months before we opened but, in practice, and given the types of students who came here, it was a bad idea. By 1975 we had a full-blown writing program.

Still many of our ideas were good ones; at least I thought so then and still do. It is those ideas that haven't been passed on and, thus, few faculty know about them today. I hope to suggest in this brief listing of the 10 things everyone should know about that there are reasons why we are the way we are.

Finally, in case you are wondering why some of the ideas are still not part of our culture, I blame the early faculty. A few simply did not accept the innovations we had put in place and wanted to replicate their graduate experience.

Grass

The original plan for the college was to use grass only on athletic fields. The campus was supposed to have been planted with native plants and grasses found in the Pine Barrens. In a recent email exchange with Richard Schwartz—the first college planner—he confirmed this plan.

Had we followed the original plan, we would not now have constant mowing—usually outside my classroom windows while I am teaching—and the resultant noise and pollution. I am uncertain why we moved so quickly to planting grass but it was everywhere around the original buildings by 1974.

Modular Construction

Given the pervasive modular construction of public (and private) buildings today, the fact that the college is constructed of modular metal panels comes as no surprise. In 1971, however, using them here was noteworthy if not unique.

First of all, the buildings were designed using a "5 foot open module." This means that anything inside the building can be changed easily. It also means that the metal used to construct the buildings was available in standard sizes; comparatively little cutting or welding was necessary thus speeding the construction process.

But there was another reason—a more subtle one—for modularity. As Richard Schwartz describes it:

... the physical plan had to meet the educational criteria, in both site and building development. Stockton's
educational plan was based on academic divisions
rather than traditional departments. Therefore individual buildings for departments were not considered,
and all of the building units were designed to be part
of one continuous facility, with each multi-use wing
or pod, connected to a central spine or gallery.

This means that our buildings can respond quickly to
changes in pedagogical design and purposes. The Founders
envisioned an institution that would change its curricular direction as needed and do so quickly. For example, as computer
technology advanced, the college could construct labs in a
variety of configurations. No one department or division had
control over space as is so often the case in older institutions.

An even better example would be the open science lab
concept which the college started with in 1971. This idea
was very new—as far as I know it was only used at one other
college in the US; there would be one big room for all science
labs. A chemistry class might meet there in the morning
and in the afternoon a physics class might use it. Each class
could set up the lab space needed by moving lab tables and
by plugging into gas/electric/water receptacles in the floor.

It sounded wonderful but, unfortunately, it didn't work in
practice. There were safety concerns, some experiments had
to be left for long periods of time, equipment storage became
a major problem and setting up took time out of the class.

Finally, the overall college design had a "street" (com-
monly called the Gallery) with classroom wings off from
that. This street would be a place to meet, buy things, eat and
commune. It would remain, but all other buildings inside
could be shaped according to academic needs.

No Chairs

There is a simple reason why the institution has no departments and departmental chairs; the Founders had had bad experiences with them. Each of us had had chairs—in the 1960s they had both budget and hiring/firing power—who abused their power. We openly sought for other ways of organizing faculty. We were, of course, not the first college to experiment with not having department chairs but we were the first in New Jersey.

Basically, we thought chairs could undemocratically influence the pedagogy, the level of faculty competence, would exacerbate class differences to control and would favor some faculty over others. We had real-life experiences to confirm these fears.

By creating elected coordinators we could produce a rather powerless office in which all members of a program would serve. We could instill in programs a democratic decision making process. We would eliminate favoritism and rank differences by insisting that all faculty work together for the common good. At the same time we shifted power up to the dean's level to whom we gave budget and hiring/firing power.

It seems to me that recent suggestions to change this arrangement to department chairs would vastly move the college into the problems we worked so hard to avoid. Some programs at the college already act like departments by allowing the coordinator to make unrestricted and un-reviewed decisions. That is never tolerated in other programs who see the value in the original arrangement.

Scattered Offices

The recent wondering about why faculty offices were not clustered around disciplines—as they are at other colleges—

almost convinced me to write a general note to the faculty explaining why. Again, it was not an accident.

The Founders' thinking was that the natural tendency for faculty is to group by discipline (or by the closest distance to mail and copy machines). Given our insistence about innovation and change, we decided that we would have "scattered offices" where faculty would be grouped by the variety of disciplines and not by one. Thus, in my first faculty office in H-Wing there was a senior psychologist next to me with a nurse on the other side. Across the hall, was a real estate expert, a very young mathematician and the nearest LITT person was well down the hallway.

I have always relished the many discussions—and a few arguments—that took place as we shared our perspectives on classroom problems, administrative actions and student silliness. More importantly, we found a community of folks whose similarities vastly outweighed their few differences.

In spite of the distances that faculty might have to walk to get mail or make copies, I suggest that this is a practice worthy of strong opposition whenever someone who doesn't understand attempts to change it.

Choice

When I was an undergraduate in the early 1960s, I had two choices—Music Appreciation or Art Appreciation—in four years. The rest of the courses I took both in the English department and in general education were chosen for me on a mimeographed piece of paper. The Founders—once again—were determined to give students as many choices as possible. Also, again, we didn't invent this idea; it was very current in the new colleges that were popping up almost every year between 1965 and 1975. One other factor, at least, was an influence as well. Students had just been allowed to drink at eighteen and were going off to Vietnam to fight. Our thinking was that if they could drink and risk dying for us, they could certainly choose among a panoply of courses.

Choice was critical for the General Studies course offerings. In the programs, we left it up to those trained in the discipline to determine which courses students needed and in which sequence.

We never kidded ourselves, however, that students would arrive at the college prepared to make intelligent choices. Thus, teaching students how to choose was a central requirement for faculty preceptors. We thought that—through questions and discussion—students could be guided to identify their interests, their goals and their abilities and from those could be guided into appropriate choices.

Precepting Was Teaching

For the Founders, it followed, therefore, that precepting was a critical and central activity and should be part of the faculty load. We envisioned preceptors seeing their students whenever there was a need; faculty would be available to assist students in whatever issues they faced at whatever time of the day—within reason, of course.

Precepting, we insisted, was advising only when students needed to actually choose courses. For example, a freshman arriving might be challenged by the question "What do you REALLY want to do?" The student might answer that she had always wanted to be a physician. Fine, we might respond, "But do you know what courses you will need to take to become a physician? Do you know how long it will take and how much money you will have to borrow?" Perhaps, the Preceptor might assign readings to get at answers for these questions or perhaps, the Preceptor might know a newly-minted MD for the freshman to talk to, etc.

Today, I doubt that discussions like these often take place. Precepting tends to be a review of program requirements (originally our Preceptees were *not* assigned to us on the basis of their interests and our discipline as they are now). We can, if asked, provide answers about how to dodge and weave through other college issues—financial aid, General Studies requirements, etc. But it is infrequent for Preceptors that I have talked with to be asked about personal problems, cultural issues, Greek Life and all of the other concerns that students have.

Faculty got credit for one teaching hour per year—one course for the four years. Once again, faculty perceived their lives as being totally devoted to students and so pushed hard for this system to be converted into the present system of advising. We have, in the past, required students to see us; now, of course, that expectation has been abandoned and it is possible for students to attend the college without ever having seen a Preceptor.

No Privilege

It is no accident that there are no faculty parking lots, faculty dining hall and other evidence of faculty rank and favoritism. The Founders saw that privilege leads to class and class leads to inequity, deference, status and, ultimately, resentment. We have managed since the beginning to keep privilege out (mostly) though every once in a while someone suggests how nice it would be if faculty had their own dining room.

We came to this conclusion as part of the insistence on democracy and equality that we laid down in 1970. Once again, we didn't invent such ideas; they were in the air and water in the 1960s. Those of us who regularly protested for both the Civil Rights and Anti-Vietnam War movements were more than suspicious of those in power who had information the rest of us didn't. As a digression, there is a direct correlation between personal computers produced in the late 1970s and the rejection of a special class of information holders of the same period.

There are concomitant practices to all of this; not only don't we have special faculty dining rooms but we are universally not called Dr. or Prof., all have the same size offices and furniture, all teach in similar classrooms and all have to follow the same procedures (generally) that students do.

No In Loco Parentis

One of the distinct aspects of the earliest Stockton—very few, if any, colleges asserted such a policy at the time—was the rejection of *in loco parentis*. When I say "rejection" I mean just that. The first president was adamant that the college was not going to act like a parent to students who could drink, vote and fight in Vietnam as adults. He said this at a time when most institutions were developing strong programs to support student life—psychological counseling, health care, financial advising, Greek Life, career counseling and other services performed by parents or high schools at home.

Bjork's thinking was clear: students were defined as adults in the larger society so the college necessarily had to reflect that definition in its policies and practices as other community agencies (e.g., police departments) also had to do.

Frankly, the Founders and the early faculty didn't see the implications of this policy at first. Some faculty and all students—and their parents—immediately raised questions. The college's admissions staff began to hear complaints from parents of prospective students that not having such services as the other State colleges was a "deal breaker" in selecting a college.

Many of the early policies were changed by faculty as I have said; this policy is an example of the market place and its wider community having a powerful influence on an early idea. Within a year or so after the opening in 1971, the college was hiring student affairs staff.

January Term

A January Term was not, of course, a new idea in 1971. Other colleges (e.g., Dartmouth) scheduled their courses this way. For us, it offered both students and faculty an opportunity to shape intensive courses off campus (January was an ideal time to fly to Europe), to create very focused courses (e.g., a study of one playwright's play culminating in attending a NY city performance) or to invent a totally new course (e.g., "The Block"—a course on oppressed sub-cultures of the central city).

The January Term was a critical aspect of the whole General Studies effort because it encouraged new course design— especially courses with some "risk," moved faculty into teaching outside of their disciplines, offered the opportunity to add activities away from the campus and, for students, confirmed "engagement."

Sadly, faculty did not like this arrangement having been used to the post-holiday time off, needing to attend professional meetings frequently held at this time and, basically, refusing to grab the opportunity to develop new courses.

The January Term was gone by 1973.

No Grades

The Founders' rejection of traditional grades was based on research that argued that very precise calculating of GPAs and other ways of numerically assessing student performance created enormous stress on students. Tragically, in some cases, this stress led to suicide. Also, our distrust of much of higher education practices in 1970 eventuated in our rejections of A F grades. Most of the new colleges of the late 1960s—e.g.,

Hampshire—had also rejected grades so the possibility was in the air.

Rejecting traditional grades was relatively easy; replacing them with some other notation was hard. Some colleges simply had Pass/Fail or Pass/No Record. This latter arrangement appealed to us and after much debate we chose it. Our variation was H–S–N. The "H" was for outstanding work. The "S" was for satisfactory work. The "N" meant no grade would be recorded for failure.

This arrangement, too, became very unpopular with faculty. What if, they asked, there was a student who wasn't doing outstanding work, yet the work was better than satisfactory? Didn't we need something (e.g., a "B" in the traditional system) between H and S? Wouldn't students, they asked, be troubled with this system because they would go from a high school record of A—everyone knew its meaning—to an H of which no one knew the significance? What if, they asked, graduate schools rejected our students because they couldn't exactly interpret what our grades meant?

The compromise proposed by the faculty was to have the students choose. For example, a student might chose A–F for courses in her major but chose H–S–N for her General Studies course. That compromise was accepted and was offered for many years until the college simply discontinued H–S–N totally because no student had chosen it.

Final Observations

I have argued for many years—indeed, I argued in the 1970s—that we needed to test these ideas for, say, a period of five years. If, after that time, members of the community (mostly faculty) still wanted to change these original policies, so be it. But, I argued, to abandon them within a few months of the college opening and, seemingly, merely because they were different from our undergraduate experiences seemed hasty and unwarranted.

Most of the aspects I've written about here were gone by 1975 at the latest. Most, not all, were rejected by the faculty. Most, in my opinion, had some merit and should have been modified but not abandoned. Most faculty at the college now know little about them yet they should because these 10 things were part of what made us distinctive and unique.

Finally, a central document in our thinking was a small booklet entitled *The Hazen Report* (1968). Briefly, this report examined the situation of the American college student in 1968 and found genuine problems. It also argued that American higher education was rapidly changing and a new university was being born which was so radically different that present institutions needed to change to meet the new student, new faculty and new academic culture. The Report deserves a new reading.

KT

The Grass is Greener on the Other Side

Here is the first of my responses to Ken's Ten Things we all should know . . .

The original conception of the college was a fine one indeed. It would have been wonderful to have the college planted with native plants and grasses found in the Pine Barrens. Had this been done from the outset, I believe a different aesthetic could have been established and might even have been award winning.

I would strongly encourage the college now experiment in this area, committing itself to making a gradual shift over to this plan, maybe making a commitment to converting a certain amount of square footage of the grounds to these alternative plantings over a period of years.

The reason that this should be a gradual process, I think, is that we are competing with other colleges who, like ourselves, cater to people who have a certain aesthetic. This is how a college should look—lots of lawns on which gentlefolk might have wonderful tea parties!

Challenging this aesthetic, and announcing that we are going on an alternate route, could work to our advantage. We could get national attention for the college if we made a grand announcement that by a certain date we would have removed grass from the college (except on the athletic fields). If we lead, others may follow, and we could even have this named the Stockton, or South Jersey, Aesthetic.

Of course, how we would handle golf courses (at the newly acquired Seaview Hotel) in such a case (even though the athletic exception was in place) would be an open question!

A final point: it would be worth actually determining how much of the campus is devoted to green lawns, and how we compare with other colleges in this regard. Looking around the campus I am struck by the fact that we have less terrain devoted to grass than many of the colleges with which I am familiar. If this impression actually reflects reality, it would be worth considering whether or not this is a result of the original vision being put in place and perhaps having an impact on what we did over the years.

RG

A Modal Construction

Here is my response to Ken's point number two.

Modular was forward looking back in 1971, and it was, as Ken notes, ahead of its time. It was flexible. I like this approach and it appeals to my own Quaker sensibility, which I think tends to highlight the beauty in function, rather than simply the beauty in appearance. It also gestures to a postmodern sensibility, one that allows for multiple entry points all of equal importance.

There are many ways through college, and each student should find his or her own way. This is a different sensibility from that at many colleges, where students find themselves consigned to different buildings, each with its own overbearing entry point. "You shall not pass, until you know the code—you need to learn the language of education before we will include you," the entry points seem to whisper. (I am reminded of a character in James Baldwin's *Go Tell it On the Mountain*, who, standing outside the New York Public Library, is somewhat intimidated by it as it is so alien to his experience.) Stockton, architecturally speaking, has said, "You are welcome here, whichever way you choose to come to us, whatever experience you bring—we will take you where we find you, and we will take you to new places."

And the main building has served Stockton very well. It has been an anchor, one that has frequently changed within as new needs have arisen. With some of the newer buildings nestled around the edges—Big Blue (or the Blauhaus, as I call it), West Quad, and the Arts & Science Building (a Michael Graves design of some note)—the main building(s) has dominated the college and helped influence how we have developed.

In this regard, the newest building (the Campus Center) has been a considerable departure. Running almost the length of the old spine and almost doubling the square footage available to us, this building promises to be transformative. Philosophically it speaks a different language—it has an entrance and it will provide different kinds of narratives for the students immediately. But do not despair, my Quaker brethren! The transformation will be there in terms of the availability of space on the campus, I believe, but it may not alter our overall sensibility. The fact is that we may all be more sophisticated now than we were in 1971; we can read and use buildings against the grain.

Moreover, colleges are now as much nestled in the mind as they are in the infrastructure. The beauty of the building will be significant, but entryways to the college will still be there in abundance—mainly found on the computer screen. Lastly, the old spine will serve us well again—and will continue to do so in the future. It will still provide us ways of creating new spaces in accordance with changing pedagogical needs, and we will continue to adjust into the future as new buildings come on line—just as happened when West Quad and Arts & Sciences were built.

RG

Sofa So Good

This is my response to Ken's point number three—regarding chairs.

So we don't have chairs. Is this a big deal? Yes and no! Yes, because it really is a good thing that we don't have multiple chairs of departments who have the ability to parcel out resources and give differential pay to people. I remember one situation I faced at another institution where the chair of the department determined what pay one received when one was hired. I learned, much to my consternation and resentment (at the time), that I was hired at a salary lower than someone hired after me with fewer qualifications. It didn't make me feel good about the place, and if that becomes the mode of operation throughout an institution, it is not a recipe for creating good feeling! So it is a big deal that we haven't created this kind of college with strong departments and autonomous chairs.

But wait! Such situations prevail largely at the big universities where there are departments (e.g., of history, language, and literature) that are sizeable indeed. Each one of the departments might be roughly a third as large as a school at Stockton. So one might suggest that our schools with their deans are comparable to departments with chairs elsewhere.

So a number of points come to mind. If we moved from coordinators to chairs, it might only mean a change in nomenclature—one that makes us more comprehensible to outsiders—rather than something more significant. Having a chair of six or seven people would mean that the person was still someone with limited power. Not much to worry about there—a pretty pathetic fiefdom even on its best day! Each program would still probably rotate their chairs in the same way that they rotate coordinators. The latter are elected and so one could have someone securing support and maintaining this position, but one doesn't because the rewards are not great. This probably wouldn't change with chairs being created.

Also, we are a union shop. Salaries are pretty much decided by external forces, and all kinds of procedures are put in place so that even a dean sometimes has less power and possibly less prestige than a chair of a large university department. This wouldn't change with the advent of chairs—whether or not someone brought a Napoleon complex or some other megalomaniacal inclination to the position.

All that said, I think keeping coordinators is a good thing, because it does speak to the uniqueness of the college. We are made up of schools and these schools do bring into connection different programs, which if they were called departments headed by chairs might be more inclined to become increasingly discipline centered. I think, for many years as a member of the history program, I would have gone along with such a move and would have wanted to create a very strong history department; but now I think some strength to that program results from it being nestled in a school of arts and humanities, and that its members teach general studies, and so forth. There is a liberation in this for members of the program—one that gives them an institutional endorsement of difference and innovation that other historians do not experience at other universities.

RG

Planned Serendipity

This is my response to Ken's point number four—regarding offices.

The issue of scattered offices has been much talked about because of the "decanting" that is about to occur as we open the new Campus Center. With the new building housing departments that were previously spread out over the main spine, there will be considerable space opening up. As such, the immediate question is how should this be filled and on the basis of what set of principles. Should we make it convenient for students and have all school offices together? Should we make each school coherent so that faculty members are clustered around their school office—with each school having its own wing? Or should we do things in a more haphazard fashion, more in line with how they were organized in the past?

Each of these plans has been considered, and certainly the first two have been rejected in part because they don't fit with the college's historical use of space. What represents convenience from the perspective of the student is something that is hard to determine, so the idea of using this as an organizing principle is perhaps of limited utility. One-stop shopping was strong in the 1990s, and this idea largely shapes the thinking behind the Campus Center, but using it throughout the college (i.e., beyond the Center) might be going to unnecessary extremes—unnecessary because students gather information on the computer and do much of the work they need to do online. Having all the school offices together might only lead to considerable congestion and frustration as everyone would be "living" and working on top of each other.

Making each school a coherent space with its own wing has numerous problems, one of which is that it goes against the founding ethos described by Ken in his piece. We do lose something when we divide into silos based upon disciplines or a cluster thereof. Stockton through its curriculum and through its interaction of people from different academic locales is a place where serendipity exists more, I believe, than elsewhere. This has been my experience at any rate.

But the original planners did not believe things would be simply haphazard—they thought that there would be possibilities for development in accordance with changing pedagogical needs, or changes occurring in the curriculum. There are reasons to put PSYC labs together, just as there are reasons to put art studios next to each other, and music practice rooms in the same area. So, as the decanting occurs, there will be some organization of the space that allows it to be used in ways that are functional to different programs or schools.

However, there will be limits to this, and the limits will be determined as much as anything by the power of property. Faculty are spread all over the main building; they are comfortable where they are (in most instances); they will not be willing to give up their spaces at the command of an administration that wants to rationalize the use of its space.

Once bureaucracies get established they don't disappear; once space gets claimed, the manner in which it has been parceled out will be hard to change. This is a good thing.

RG

The Chosen Ones

This is the response to Ken's point number five.

If the founders of the college intended to provide students with choice once they got to Stockton, it should still be recognized as a pillar of this institution. Many freshmen come to the college without having chosen a major and choose only after having taken many different courses. The flexibility of the curriculum is one of its strongest features and makes it unique in the academy.

This is not less true with regard to transfer students. These students, at least those who have the Associates degree, have had two years already to decide what they will major in. By the time they arrive at Stockton, they have decided and they often take the fastest route through the college they can find. This must have been the case for transfer students in the early years as well. Ironically the complexity of the curriculum, which almost requires experimentation for the freshman, has the potential to be a straight-jacket for the transfer student. Such choice, then, has been a privilege shared by those who come to the college soon after the completion of their high school careers.

There may be some difference between now and what occurred during the college's early days, however, with regard to the fact that where choice exists it is most likely that decisions will not occur in conjunction with the advising or precepting process. Indeed, advising is most frequently something that occurs primarily after choices have been made, and the advisor is now someone who understands the intricacies of a particular major, rather than someone who provides guidance about the college and beyond. The student is more likely to decide on a major based upon success—and, somewhat relatedly, based upon the course that he or she liked and the teacher who inspired them.

There is no doubt that the college has become more discipline oriented. Where choice exists, it is between majors, even if there are interdisciplinary routes into each one and a multiplicity of offerings for students to savor beyond the major that they decide upon.

I would suggest that one reason for this is found in the decline of the LIBA—the Liberal Arts degree. This started out as a major that allowed students to determine what their degree should look like. Through a precepting process they would begin to determine the courses they needed to take to achieve their objectives. In some instances, a student attempted to work in an area where there was no major being offered at the college; in others, the student fashioned a degree from a wide array of disciplinary and interdisciplinary offerings that they felt they could justify to the faculty as worthy of a degree. This was choice taken to its highest level.

The trouble was that it died—for all intents and purposes. It became a Cadillac (Rolls Royce, even) degree that very few Stockton students were considered able to accomplish—an un-Stocktonian notion if ever there was one. If only three or four people per year were taking this path to the BA, then it could hardly be said to exist as a Stockton degree.

Fortunately, I believe we are close to returning to our roots and establishing a degree that will accomplish what the LIBA did in the early years. We have been working hard to establish a BAIS degree—a Bachelor of Interdisciplinary Studies. This will return choice and flexibility to the curriculum; it will allow those who are not meeting the requirements of a particular major to create something different; it will allow those who have left and been stuck a few credits from a degree to return and achieve what they couldn't accomplish years ago; it will cater to the non-traditional student thereby allowing many new groups of people to experience the wonders of a Stockton education.

Simply put, education is not about catering to the chosen ones; each individual should have choice, and each student should feel that he or she is able to choose their own route to the goal he or she is striving to reach. That should be Stockton's mission—to provide that opportunity for the people of Southern New Jersey.

RG

Advising is Teaching II

My response to Ken's point number six.

As Ken notes, in the early days of the college precepting was considered teaching and there was some workload credit given for it. It was supposed to be more significant than the kind of advising we now do. Yet, while there may have been considerable opportunity for providing the student with a unique experience, one wonders, again, whether this was felt by all students equally. The freshman would have gained a great deal more from the precepting experience than the transfer student. But, perhaps we should say, that was the benefit of coming to Stockton straight away and not stopping at a community college for two years. Perhaps this needs further articulation, as we endeavor to make it clear to the transfer student what they need to accomplish at Stockton—and it needs to be part of a strong Transfer Seminar program.

Isn't it interesting that we have a freshman seminar and a freshman year experience, but really do not have the same thing for transfer students. What is the reason for this? It is about retention and engaging students immediately so that they don't leave and go to another institution. And these things work well. We don't worry about transfer students so much, because they will be taking the fastest route through the college and it is unlikely that they will leave us. No worry—no services!

But it is nonetheless true that, from the perspective of inculcating values, it is perhaps more important to reach the transfer student than the freshman. The latter has a longer period in which to imbibe the spirit of the college; he or she has a greater opportunity to experiment; heck, he or she gets his or her own freshman seminar! By the time they reach their junior year, we hope that they have experienced our General Studies courses, and that they have been taught to question and articulate their own ideas. Meanwhile, the transfer student is experiencing a much more traditional education—a continuation in many respects of the approaches he or she was encumbered with in high school. Listen and repeat, listen and repeat; know facts. Don't think about interpretations. We only get the transfer students at Stockton for two to three years—perhaps we should spend more energy trying to help them learn what we think college should be all about...!

But I digress. An extreme understatement, since I am supposed to be talking about Precepting. So let's find our way back, if we can.

It seems to me that precepting is more important than we give it credit for being. We have shrunk it down to advising for the major, and we assume that all students understand what these majors are and how they should achieve success in them. We have created a Banner system that allows students to go through their careers advising themselves, more or less. Where precepting used to be compensated, there is now no support for faculty who do the job well. We talk about advising being teaching—but the bottom line is that we pay for teaching, while we don't pay for advising. What do we expect?

Even if we now advise, where we might have precepted before—and we might want to consider the Wilsonian and Princetonian origin of the latter term and therefore its potential elitism—we should be endeavoring to build an advising system that is course and workload based. I only have the haziest notion of how this might be accomplished at the moment, but I think we need to tie it more firmly into the curriculum.

Since the majority of our students are transfers and since they are more program-based than the four-year students (and given that the four-year students will have received a mentoring through the freshman seminar system), we should perhaps privilege the transfers in our thinking and tie to each major an advising course that begins in the second year and is linked to the capstone courses (e.g. the thesis). I worry that we may lose some interdisciplinarity here, but if we get a robust Bachelor of Interdisciplinary Studies, located in the office of advising, we could perhaps revive the whole advising process at the college.

That's my second plug in one night for this new/old Stockton degree.

RG

On Being Impractical—
Walls, Ticket-Takers and Kings

These remarks were delivered at the 2010 Graduation Ceremony of Richard Stockton College of New Jersey on December 19, 2010.

Among all of the crises we face each day, the crisis in and about the Humanities is surely way down on the list. In an absolute sense, if there was a crisis in the Humanities, it's one where no lives are lost, no financial empires fall and no moral fiber is weakened.

Yet, in our lives, jobs have been lost, people have been changed, potentials haven't been realized and the future has been affected. There seems, then, to be a disconnect between all that comes under the word "Humanities" and our lives.

The problem is that, as Americans, we think we believe in the practical; we say "It's good if it is practical." We think we believe this but we don't, of course.

For example, there is nothing practical when Americans spend $166 billion a year on alcohol, $157 billion on smoking, $110 billion on illicit drugs, $107 billion on overeating and $40 billion on gambling. These astonishing figures not only include the actual cost of the addiction but also the cost of treatment.

These are hardly "practical" values. Their effect is momentary pleasure and, ultimately, pain.

So, we argue that we see no value in engaging in the Arts or the Humanities. When school budgets are cut in America, the art and music classes go first. Others quickly follow.

The idea that anything connected with the Humanities must have practical value—and if it doesn't we invent it—can be shown from an experience I had when I was in college; I was required to take either art or music appreciation. When I asked my advisor why these two courses—I was an English major and he was a Physics teacher—I was informed quite abruptly that those sorts of courses were "good for you" and would "improve your life." I learned, of course, that this was simply claptrap.

Strangely, we don't make the same arguments about science courses. I assume that only hardcore math or physics teachers would ever say that a course in Calculus is "good for you" or that a course in Physics at the Atomic Level will "improve your life"!

I want to suggest, then, that for the purposes of these remarks, we abandon the idea that the Humanities have any "practical" value and, instead, concentrate on the clear values—even if they are impractical—that they do provide.

What values, then, *do* the Humanities give us?

(Parenthetically, the idea that they give us values is itself problematic. "Giving us value" implies that we can measure those values. We can perform such measurements in the sciences. If a scientist invents a new compound, one of the first results is to estimate what and how much value will be returned on the investment. This, I believe, is impossible in the humanities and when it is done, it returns false data. How, for example, could I possibly numerically measure how or whether a Shakespearean play might have meaning to one of my students?)

Without trying to measure the impact or value of the Humanities we can, and many have, suggest broad ways that the arts and humanities can be important in our lives. Because they offer these insights, they should be regarded as significant and, thus, worthy of support.

My closest friend—Professor Wendel White—recently sent me a document written in 1964 which was the result of a national study of the role of the Humanities. I think he sent it to me knowing how desperately I have been struggling with this speech and because the conclusions in the document were current and important when we founded the college. I would like to believe that these ideas can still be found at Stockton and can be seen in the curricula, in our assumptions about students, in the mission of the college and even in the design of the early buildings. More, perhaps, on this later.

The document concludes with the following observations:

- America needs a national ideal for which to strive; the Humanities can provide it.
- Our democracy demands wisdom from its citizens; the Humanities can offer it.
- While we believe that we are a nation of materialists, the Humanities consistently tell us we are not.
- World leadership cannot merely be about superior force, vast wealth or dominating technologies; it must be about leadership based on elements of the spirit.
- Americans have enormous amounts of leisure time and the humanities can make this time more significant.

These are all laudable and critical goals. Even though they were written 50 years ago, I have no trouble agreeing and supporting them.

But the Humanities are only secondarily about democracy, the nation and the world. For me, the Humanities are about us—individual humans trying to understand who we are, what we are capable of and why we are here. These, too, are laudable and critical goals.

I want to spend the rest of our time together telling you about how I personally see the critical importance of the Humanities and giving you examples of my experiences teaching them for 40 years.

First of all, and I don't want to be blasphemous here, but teaching is a kind of religion to me and it has one commandment—strive to find out what it means to be human. I devoutly believe that humans and, therefore, human life have meaning. It is my task to convince students of this and to help them pull the meaning from literary life and, by extension, expose the meaning of their lives as well. We don't, therefore, read just for meaning; we read for us.

You and I—the "us" I just mentioned—live at Stockton in a physical and intellectual environment steeped in Humanistic values. They are terribly practical here and, I submit, essential to a meaningful life. I cannot imagine Stockton without them. Let me see if I can explain.

You may have noticed, if you have been here long, that the college is constructed out of metal panels and that those panels can be changed at any time. Every wall throughout the older buildings can be taken down and raised again in a different configuration. While this made the original construction easier, it also made it possible—unlike traditional buildings where walls cannot be moved—for the building to match human needs. If we decided that we needed smaller classrooms, we could partition off a larger room into smaller rooms. Simple. Human needs should change buildings.

Those who created the college (I among them) were also convinced that privilege was a detriment to learning; inequalities caused class resentments and we can't learn if we feel suppressed and unheard. Perhaps you haven't noticed but there are no faculty parking lots, no faculty dining rooms or faculty lounges. Students routinely call me by my first name; Doctor and Professor are seldom heard. When I was an undergraduate, I saw the president twice in four years and I wouldn't have thought about trying to meet with him. Our president can be seen everywhere on campus and will chat with you if his advice is needed.

Perhaps the most important of these Humanistic values here at Stockton is choice. Stockton students have an enormous range of choices compared to other institutions. You can choose classes, which days of the week to be on campus, preceptors, where to eat, where to park and even what to wear. When I was an undergraduate, all men wore sports coats and ties, women wore dresses, I had almost no choices of classes, when I would be on campus, where I would park or where I would eat.

The choices you have here may not seem important but let me assure you that they are. Choice was a fundamental value when we founded the college; our early documents are full of discussions about the need for choice and how having choices will better prepare you for your lives when you leave the college.

My point is that values that center on the human *can be* practical, are democratic and allow us all to learn about ourselves in powerful ways.

I want to close with some comments about a short story and a tragedy; both illustrate powerfully "what it means to be human."

One of my favorite texts is a short story by Bernard Malamud called "Idiots First." In this story a father (Mendel) has a mentally challenged son (Isaac) and he is desperately trying to find someone who will take care of his son after his death. You see, he has been visited by Death (Ginzburg) and was told that he has just a few hours to live. Mendel visits three friends—a pawnbroker, a rich man and a rabbi—begging each to take his son and care for him. All refuse.

Finally, Mendel decides to send his son by train to California to his brother who will, indeed, care for Isaac. The problem is: will he get him on the train before Death appears? After much frustration they arrive at the train station but Death is there—as a ticket-taker—blocking their way. The train is close by and ready to leave but Death will not let Mendel and Isaac pass. I quote Malamud:

> Mendel, in a burst of rage, grabs Death and says: "You dog you." Mendel lunged at Ginzsburg's throat and began to choke. "You Bastard, don't you understand what it means human?"

Ginzburg is unrelenting, but at the moment of Mendel's death, Malamud writes:

> Clinging to Ginzburg in his last agony, Mendel saw reflected in the ticket collector's eyes the depth of his terror. But he saw that Ginzburg, staring at himself in Mendel's eyes, saw mirrored in them the extent of his own awful wrath. He beheld a shimmering, starry, blinding light that produced darkness.

Death understands at that moment what it means to be human and the awful power being human has to accept and forgive and also to resist. This is what the humanities offer us—the most profound insights into what it means to be human.

The tragedy I want to mention is Shakespeare's *King Lear*—a play with which I have wrestled for 40 years because it seems to me that this play—as difficult and as terrifying as it is—also offers some final, profound insights into what it means to be human.

Shakespeare wrote *The Tragedy of King Lear* sometime between 1603 and 1606. It is one of his last plays and is, arguably, his greatest work. The plot is fairly simple. Lear, at the beginning, is old and to prevent civil strife among his daughters after his death, offers to divide the kingdom for each daughter on the basis of how much they love him. The eldest two of his daughters declare their love; the youngest cannot and so is banished.

Lear, who has arranged to spend long periods of time with each daughter, is rejected by both and is driven from safety into the wilderness. There he has periods of madness blaming his two daughters for his fate. Eventually, in the depths of insanity, he is rescued by the invasion of his youngest daughter coming to save him. His sanity returns but in the final terrifying scene his youngest daughter dies just before he does.

All tragic heroes—either by their own arrogance or by others' power—abandon family, responsibility and culture. They reject being connected in favor of the isolation of their pride.

If the play was a comedy, Lear would start being isolated and disconnected and end up integrated into a large community. But, of course, the play isn't a comedy. Lear must experience isolation, loss, disconnection as a King so he can learn the value of the Human. Ironically, being a Human is exactly what he has forgotten and, yet, what he thinks he has an abundance of. The early Lear insists that he is gracious, generous, tolerant—all human traits—but, in fact, he is petty, rash and ignorant of his situation. It is that humanness that he must learn.

He also utterly rejects failure and error. It is, he asserts again and again, his daughters' ingratitude (they are, by the way, Shakespeare's finest harpies) that is the cause of his fall. His errors, misjudgments and blindness to the Truth cause him to falter but he maintains his innocence about such failures until almost the end.

In addition, he cannot imagine that he might be wrong because to do so would, he believes, destroy himself. He is safe in the present and demands that it continue without change. As he is abandoned by his daughters, he, more importantly, abandons Self and, finally, abandons Reason—the one trait that signifies our humanness.

Lear's fall is not the result of being too human but of being too little human. As King, he has forgotten that rule long before the play opens. If he is to come to an understanding of his condition, he must lose himself to gain himself. As all good LITT majors know: you've got to go down to go up.

The terror for the tragic hero—and, by extension, for us—is explained by Lear's experiences. We are afraid that we will lose ourselves in trying to preserve ourselves. Lear, in the middle of the play, begins to understand this though he cannot bring himself to accept it. What if, in fighting the Human, we become inhuman?

The fact is we need other humans. We need to recognize that in this society where error and failure are considered almost sinful, accepting them aids us in becoming more human. We also need not to be afraid—as we certainly are these days—of what we don't know, of what we can't understand, of what we haven't experienced. We need to see that fear will keep us from becoming the humans we need to be. This is what I try to teach, this is what literature teaches and it is what the Humanities teach.

Lear does not understand what it means to be human. He rejects the human as inadequate, inappropriate, faltering, error-prone and ridiculous. But finally he sees being human as transcendent, powerful, absolutely capable and, ultimately, loving.

Ah, there it is! At the center of being human when we are least deserving of that word, the possibility of love is offered. Being human is to love and to be worthy of love. How simple and how profound.

KT

Standing On Shoulders

I am not an organized person. I wish I were but there it is . . .
I am not an organized person. It's not that I haven't tried—I've
had lists in leather bound journals, lists on computers, lists in
computer databases and in software specifically designed to keep
track of personal possessions. But they never work out for me.

On the other hand, I am not like the Collyer Brothers. I
do have file cabinets and boxes where, if I look long enough
and patiently enough, I usually find what I need. Right now,
for example, I have lost an obituary of my great-grandfather.
It would help if I could remember whether it had been sent to
me as a postal letter or it had been sent as an email attachment.
I have an email database going back to the late 1990, so it will
be there if I received it as an email and if I can figure out the
search word I need to get a hit. If it was sent via postal mail,
then I should be looking through the papers on most of the
flat surfaces in my computer room. I've done both but it hasn't
revealed its whereabouts.

I have a retired colleague who should be given a national
prize for organization. In 1971, he and his family left Texas to
take a job at the brand new Stockton. The contents of his house
had been loaded onto a commercial moving van while he and
his family drove to New Jersey by car. They got here a couple
of days before the moving van so were living off the floor of
their new home.

A day or so after they arrived here, a man knocked on their
door, identified himself as a claims adjuster for the moving

company and informed them that on the trip from Texas the moving van had caught fire and burned to the ground! All of their household goods were gone. He then explained that he could replace the cost of the lost furniture on an average family of my colleague's former home and family size.

My colleague asked what the insurance company would need to reimburse exactly what was lost? The reply was: accurate lists of every object, its condition, preferably with a photograph as well as original sales slips for major appliances as well as the dates of purchase. My colleague went into another room and returned with a large cardboard box; he opened it and produced folders for each room of his house in Texas with photos of each item along with sales slips for most of them.

The adjustor was astounded; he reported that he had never seen such set of documents and promptly covered the loss in full.

I also suspect that my colleague could provide any assignment, test or writing topics for any class that he had ever taught. He is, without question, the most organized person I know.

All this is preface to the fact that my wife handed me a stack of mimeographed pages today that she found in an old file cabinet she was emptying. I quickly glanced through them realizing immediately that they were from the chairman of the English department where I had my first full-time teaching job in 1965–1967. As I worked through the stack, I saw agendas of English department meetings, proposals for an Honors program, curricular redesigns and, best of all, a four-page document entitled *Some Comments on General Education*—3 October 1964, written by Wes Tilley.

The date is important because it is some months *before* I had accepted a teaching position at Millikin University. The date is six years before the founding of Stockton and my involvement as the first Dean of General Studies.

I quickly read the four pages and realized that what I held in my hands was a document antecedent to the thinking about general education that had so occupied me for fifteen months between July 1970 and September 1971 when the college opened.

I have mentioned here recently what the influence of Wes Tilley was on me when he was my first chairman at Millikin in 1965 and, subsequently, here at Stockton when he was the first VP of Academic Affairs. He mentored me in all sorts of ways—pedagogically, politically, culturally—as a new, young, almost Ph.D. teacher.

One of the primary topics of our (almost constant) discussions was general education. The idea of General Studies at Stockton was a compilation of Wes Tilley's ideas (precisely expressed in the 1964 document) and my very early ideas about how to make the whole thing work.

The germs of what we eventually created at Stockton vis-a-vis General Studies are in the 1964 document. It is those four pages I want to outline here.

The document contains nine "comments" suggesting a basic general education theory as well as practice for a college (specifically Millikin but meant also for wider communities). It covers the need for choice, advising principles, instructor effectiveness and the design of inter-disciplinary courses. The center of the argument discusses the content of interdisciplinary courses and how a teacher would, necessarily, teach in such courses. Needless to say, teaching in an interdisciplinary course was, Tilley argues, radically different from teaching in a major/disciplinary course.

The specifics:

At the heart of everything Wes Tilley thought about was "choice." He devoutly believed that without choice not much learning took place. His writings at Stockton—the *Academic Working Papers*, *Goals at Stockton* (both of these have been discussed and analyzed extensively here), and other memos— consistently argue for providing choice, challenging choice, encouraging choice and learning through choice.

In this document, Comment One states:

> Students usually profit more from academic require-
> ments if, within the requirements, they are permitted
> to make some choices for themselves. I hope we can
> offer every freshman first a choice between disciplinary
> and interdisciplinary courses; second, some choices
> among courses of either kind.

Numbering this one clearly shows the centrality of the idea.

Students, he argues, cannot make good and informed choices unless they have guidance—from an advisor. Thus, his second comment states:

> In advising a student, it is helpful to keep in mind that
> he may have no clear idea of the nature of an inter-
> disciplinary course. He should be discouraged from
> choosing such a course merely because he does not
> like the disciplinary courses that he would otherwise
> be required to take. The students who seem to do best
> in interdisciplinary courses are (1) the more intelli-
> gent, and (2) those with the wider range of interests.
> Those who do best in disciplinary courses are (1) older
> students, and (2) those with the more clearly defined
> goals and predilections.

While we might find Tilley's insistence that intelligent students do better in interdisciplinary courses troubling, he would most likely counter that it takes a particular and broad view of the self and the world to appreciate the range of ideas in a truly interdisciplinary course.

If students need choice, instructors need to teach what they are interested in. Tilley states in the third comment:

> Instructors are most effective when they teach the kinds of courses they like to teach. It would be essential to a sound program of general education that it permit each faculty member to teach disciplinary or interdisciplinary courses as he preferred.

This seems fundamental but only because at Stockton faculty have the freedom to choose which courses they will teach—especially in the General Studies curriculum. This is not true at other, more traditional institutions where beginning faculty are told what they are to teach. In such institutions, a departmental syllabus is quite common.

Tilley then turns his attention to what an interdisciplinary course is, how it is structured and what some possible courses might look like.

Here are the next three comments (Numbers Four, Five, Six):

> 4. It is important to keep in mind, when devising inter-disciplinary courses, that they can more easily combine materials than methods: in a course combining historical, philosophical, and literary works, there is likely to be some sacrifice of two disciplines, so that what emerges will be either a history course with literary and philosophical illustrations, a literature

course in which history and philosophy figure as types of literature, or a philosophy course in which literary and historical works are examined for their ideas. (Even when the materials are combined by a committee, the different kinds of courses will be determined by the disciplines of the various instructors.)

5. There has been a tendency in some institutions to try to decide the content of interdisciplinary courses by committees, as if once the contents were decided, everyone could teach the same course; This procedure handicaps the teacher of an interdisciplinary course so badly, it is hard to see why anyone would support it, unless he wanted the course not to succeed. It should be recognized that no one teaches well who does not feel able to devise his own courses, or free to change them as his training, his interests, and the nature of particular classes seem to indicate he should.

6. From these remarks it will be clear that I do not wish to restrict the teacher of an Interdisciplinary course in any unnecessary way—and that, further, I do not believe that a teacher should be any less free to determine the nature of an interdisciplinary course than of a disciplinary one. What form, then, should interdisciplinary course offerings take at Millikin?

Finally, in the final comment, Tilley argues for an honest "ignorance" on the part of the faculty teaching an interdisciplinary course. This "ignorance" is a fact because no faculty can master two different disciplines so it is best to admit this up front and then use the occasion as an opportunity for both the faculty and the students to learn. Here is what Tilley says:

Pedagogically, the main difference between interdisciplinary courses and disciplinary ones is that an interdisciplinary course, calling as it does upon a variety of disciplines, will not permit an instructor to take the role of masterdisciplinarian. He must necessarily confess his ignorance of much that pertains to the materials under examination and enter into something like a Socratic relationship with his students. Teachers who do not wish to teach in this way, or who are inclined to regard regular interchanges between instructor and students as mere conversation, or as "a pooling of ignorance" probably should not teach interdisciplinary courses. The instructor of an interdisciplinary course should be chosen, not for his knowledge of, say, the novel, or of Victorian literature, but for his general knowledge, his interest in broad questions, and his ability to carry on a reasoned dialogue with his students. These remarks do not necessarily prescribe "discussion" technique of teaching: they suggest the attitude of a good interdisciplinary instructor toward his materials and his students. He may talk most of the time or he may not: but when he does talk, he expresses the results, not of specialized training and research, but broad learning and a reasoned examination of the materials in the course.

I want, now, to turn to how these ideas have manifested themselves in Stockton's approach to general education. Tilley's comments contain the minimal but central ideas that he—and, then, I—implemented in our General Studies curriculum.

First of all, I was as clear as Tilley is about the need for choice in course selection. It is as central to my thinking as it was to his. I originally placed no restrictions on the selection of

GS courses; it was a smorgasbord of possibilities. I did create minimal categories but, primarily, as an administrative means of identifying course content; it was never—at that point—a distribution requirement. These came later.

Choice at Stockton meant—as it meant to Tilley—someone to guide those choices; in our case, that person was the Preceptor. The Preceptor was central to the process of choosing. Her task was to help the student—using Socratic questioning—to identify interests which would lead to informed choice of courses.

The third leg of this stool was the instructor. Teaching in the General Studies curriculum was a contractual obligation. Each faculty was to teach two courses per academic year in GS. I assumed at the beginning that the best GS courses would be, somehow, interdisciplinary.

For example, in the interview process with new candidates, I would ask what courses they might like to teach in GS. Usually, the response would be conservative. Thus, a sociologist almost always replied with a course very much like SOC 101. I would then counter by stating some of the ways a GS course might be created and structured. The example I would give was a course that I have always wanted to teach. I called it "1381." This course, centered on one year, would include literature (*The Canterbury Tales*), history (The Peasants Revolt), politics (The Deposing of Richard II), art (Building Westminster Abbey) and any other cultural material I could find that occurred in 1381.

Almost always, the candidate would immediately see that Stockton was no usual place, that we not only desired but required new ideas and that I was eager to hear about any course they had up their sleeves. Indeed, almost all actually had such courses up their sleeves but weren't sure I would welcome them.

From this point in the conversation, the faculty candidate and I spoke the same tongue and could actually design workable GS courses in my office. These discussions were exhilarating to both of us.

Faculty who could not get outside of their disciplinary box did not get positive references from me. Certain disciplines seemed to be harder to shed than others. As Tilley argues, these faculty should not teach interdisciplinary courses.

I am amazed that this unimpressive mimeographed document has survived two moves of my family, 50 years of passing time, to end up in an old file cabinet on my front porch. Without it, we would still understand Tilley's and my initial ideas about General Studies. With it, however, it is clear that this cluster of ideas is much older than what we have and that those ideas are directly traceable to this document.

I stand on shoulders far greater than mine.

KT

First of the First

A few days ago when going through some papers in a file, I found a copy of an *Atlantic City Press* article from January 9, 1971, which has the headline: "11 Professors Hired By Stockton College." The article lists the names, official titles and salaries of the group. Wes Tilley—the first VP of Academic Affairs—is quoted as pointing out that this group of 11 brings the total number of faculty hired to 20. This is one third of the projected total faculty of 55.

As I read the article, I wondered who the first faculty hired was. This sent me to the college Archives and to Louise Tillstrom, the incredibly helpful Assistant Archivist. I asked Louise if she would try to find the exact dates and names of the faculty appointments in the Minutes of the board of trustees. She spent a goodly part of the morning searching through the Minutes and found all of the appointments of the First Cohort of 55 faculty.

Before I provide the listing and try to answer the question of who was the first appointee, I want to review our recruitment plans and procedures.

The founding deans worked through the summer of 1970 setting up policies, organizational structures and academic definitions for programs, governance, divisions and disciplines. It was clear to us that with all of this in place we would then need to hire faculty to flesh out the work of that summer. To make sure that we had requisite faculty, we began recruiting in the early Fall of 1970. Our goal was to have the faculty hired by the Spring of 1971, when they would be involved in the details of the curricula during that Summer in preparation for opening in the Fall of 1971.

The first recruitment ad for the college was placed in *Academe* in June of 1970. It started with this paragraph:

> Richard Stockton State College of New Jersey: Scheduled to open with 500 students in September, 1971; will accept applications for faculty positions all levels for the 1971–72 academic year. A new and rapidly developing institution, Stockton will encourage innovation and experimentation in the undergraduate (and later, graduate) curriculum. Stockton should appeal most to the teaching scientist or scholar who is interested in shaping exceptionally sound and significant programs. Located just outside Atlantic City, Stockton will offer the advantages of comfortable living and convenient access to Philadelphia and New York. Salaries will be competitive with most institutions.

This was followed by a description and contact information of each division. Here is an example for the Social and Behavioral Sciences:

> The Division of Social and Behavioral Sciences will include the disciplines of Political Science, Economics, Sociology, Anthropology, and Psychology. The division will use new interdisciplinary methods to define and attack a variety of urban and environmental problems. For further information please write to W. H. Tilley, Vice President for Academic Affairs, Richard Stockton State College, Pleasantville, New Jersey 08232.

By the Fall of 1970, the ad had been rewritten, Wes Tilley's name had been replaced by Woody Thrombley—the first dean of the division—and the description had been rewritten (it would seem that Tilley wrote the first but the second version was changed by Thrombley).

> The Division of Social and Behavioral Sciences will include the disciplines of Political Science, Economics, Sociology, Anthropology, and Psychology. The division will seek to develop new interdisciplinary methods and approaches to ensure the kind of horizontal integration of curriculum which we feel is an essential complement to the customary vertical integration of the departmental major. For further information, please write to W. G. Thrombley, Chairman, Division of Social and Behavioral Sciences, Richard Stockton State College, Pomona, New Jersey 08240.

There are other changes between the first ad and the second. The Division of General Studies omitted from the first has been added to the second. Originally, when I interviewed for the position in March 1970, I was not going to have any staff. By the time I had arrived in July, that decision had been changed and General Studies was going to have an initial staff of six, so text was added to the recruitment ad placed later in the Summer of 1970.

The deans (actually, we were officially designated as chairmen but that is another tale) actively recruited in the Fall of 1970.

To structure and universalize our recruitment practices, Wes Tilley wrote a five page document in August, 1970. The document outlines where we would place ads:

- *Placement Offices of Major Universities*
- *Professional Colleagues of Established Reputations*
- *Chairmen of Graduate Departments*
- *Notices in Professional Journals*
- *Commercial Agencies*

There is nothing terribly different in the listing from a national search today, but it does illustrate the bed from which we were going to pluck flowers.

Our overall schedule—a very detailed, hour-by-hour interview schedule also included in the document—was as follows:

- During October and November [1970] we should aim to fill about one-third of our projected positions, giving priority to projected majors.
- During January and February we should aim to fill another two-thirds.
- During April and May we should be able to fill most of the assigned positions. It may be necessary, however, to keep several positions unassigned, in order to meet the pattern of late enrollments.

When the candidates finally arrived on campus, we were to consider them within the following general purposes:

- We want the candidate to get a sense of the academic community, and of the larger community which it must serve.
- We want an opportunity to hear at length from the candidate, in order to assure ourselves that both the faculty and the students will be able to work with him toward the established goals of the

180

institution, and that he will be able to do his share in the development of outstanding programs.

- We want an opportunity to acquaint the candidate with our ways of thinking and with our previous decisions, so that during the interval before he joins the faculty he will be able to think constructively about his future on our campus.

It should be noted that (1) we had made previous decisions during the twelve months leading up to this moment. It has been claimed by some early faculty that we "over sold" the new college by suggesting that everyone's input would have significance. (2) that we wanted evidence from our discussions with candidates that they really liked students, especially state college students. In addition, we sought faculty who wanted to build programs (read: departments), curricula, policies, etc. Not all did, especially those who came to us directly from the most famous and most scholarly institutions. (3) We also wanted candidates to understand that there were many communities at the college, including actual communities in the environs and that our expectation was that they served all of them.

The document concludes with the "principles of faculty selection" that we were to employ:

- Our first consideration must be pedagogical excellence. This would be a simple requirement if it were not so easy to confuse with popularity.
- It is essential that the candidate show an interest in teaching the kinds of students we shall probably have at Stockton.
- It is also essential that the candidate show outstanding intellectual, scientific, or artistic ability and very desirable that he show at least two of these.

- While long lists of publications are suspect, the candidate ought to show a serious interest in the continuing inquiry that is properly called research, if he is to teach effectively in a serious institution. (We encounter a paradox here: people who are not interested in doing or at least in aiding research seldom make good teachers; but what is usually called research is more often the grinding out of routine operations or, especially in the humanities, the spinning out of undisciplined cerebrations: and this kind of thing does not make for intellectual scientific, or artistic leadership—which is to say, does not make for good teaching.)
- We should pay careful attention to the probable capacity of a candidate to work in flexible and open situations. (The kind of candidate who keeps to himself and wants to work only with his chairman may find Stockton unpleasant, if not unendurable.)
- Because we are placing so much emphasis on the interactions of faculty and of faculty and students, the candidate should show that he is able to carry on a productive academic discussion.
- Finally, somewhere in the candidate's experience there should be a period of several years during which he has worked or taught in a first-class institution.

There are significant expectations in this list. Notice, first, that teaching was the absolute criterion. In addition, notice that traditional scholarship is doubted as a litmus for good teaching. Evidence of scholarship is also suspect—not because Tilley thought that it might have been falsified or plagiarized—but because, if a candidate presented a long list of articles, chapters, books and other scholarly writings, he created that list at the cost of teaching. For Tilley one couldn't have both.

It is also clear that Tilley and the founding deans understood completely what sorts of students Stockton was going to attract. This is significant because there are critics who argue that the early Stockton faculty was blinded about the sorts of students we were going to attract here and, therefore, were shocked and dismayed when students actually appeared. The college may have been jokingly named "Princeton in the Pines" but we all understood that we were not ever going to live up to that title; nor did we want to!

We also were in agreement that Stockton was and would be in flux and that faculty had to delight in change and impermanence. I have, for example, written elsewhere about the pedagogical values implicit in the fact that all of the walls of the college were modular and could be changed easily and quickly into other configurations. The shape of the college was impermanent not for architectural reasons, but the architecture was shaped by pedagogical demands. We wanted faculty not only to understand this, but to seek it.

There is an implied (not very covertly) collegiality in these desiderata. Faculty connections to other faculty and to students was expected. We distrusted candidates who displayed tendencies to isolation or who showed contempt for students. We wanted, and generally got, faculty who had had very positive experiences with students and who would treat students as equals. This was particularly true about the science faculty though it pertained across all of the divisions.

Tilley closes with an acerbic comment on other institutions; let me hasten to add that, generally, the deans totally agreed with Tilley on these issues so we did not, at the time, find them distasteful or wrong.

Please remember that the point of all these comments is just to help us find scientists, scholars, artists, and intellectuals who will teach in both an exciting and a responsible way. It seems vitally important that we work together to bring that kind of academician to Stockton. No doubt mistakes will occur. But in the long run, if we keep the objective in mind, we shall probably succeed—if only because most colleges and universities have other objectives, or have lost sight of their objectives, or still do not know what their objectives ought to be.

The recruiting process started with ads. The next step was to send the four deans forth into the country to interview interested candidates. Each of us was assigned a "territory" and we spent a week or more going from university to university interviewing candidates: most of whom were graduate students.

I went to the Midwest visiting Chicago, Ohio, Indiana, Illinois and Iowa. While exhausting, these trips gave us an opportunity to gauge interest, to find out where our descriptions of the college and the position needed tweaking, to report back on where it was going to be easy and hard to recruit specific disciplines. We all came back with lists of candidates and suggestions for sharpening and clarifying our presentation of the college.

All of this effort paid off;—we received 5300 applications for 55 positions!

Here are some stats that may be of interest:

- Among the 56 First Cohort there were 11 Professors, 10 Associates, 30 Assistants and 5 Instructors.
- The average age was 32.6

- The number of doctorates was 30
- The number of doctorates expected was 21
- The number of women was 7
- The number of African-Americans was 3

The faculty was born in 19 different states and 5 foreign nations. Based upon the place of recent employment, the faculty came from 21 public colleges and universities, 22 private colleges and universities, 10 public agencies and 3 private concerns.

The doctorates earned by the faculty were granted by 27 different institutions.

The first group of 5 faculty presented to the board of trustees was on December 9, 1970. They were Enscoe, Hecht, Marsh, Mench and Solo.

On January 7, 1971 a second group of 11 were presented. They were Broughton, Constantelos, Decker, Klein, Lacy, Lester, Lubenow, Mikulak, John Miller, Reiss and Wirth.

A third group of six was presented in February 11, 1971. They were Daly, Epstein, Jaffe, Milstein, Rickert and Townsend.

On March 4, 1971 Bean, Ferrell, Ford, Loft, Steinberg, Wilmore were presented. It was the fourth group of six.

The fifth group of 17 was presented on April 6, 1971. They were Bogart, Colby, Falk, Good, Haggerty, Hartzog, Helsabeck, Larsen, Manley, Marino, Ozersky, Plank, Richert, Richey, Sanford, Sternfeld and Wood.

On May 18, 1971, the sixth group of ten was presented to the board of trustees. They were Bailey, Burkman, Drummond, Gilmore, Martin Miller, Silverman, Smith, Sorkin, Stanton and Taylor.

Interestingly enough, out of this First Cohort of 55 only seven remain at the college teaching full time. They are Daly, Epstein, Farrell, Helsabeck, Lester, Lubenow and Wood.

So who was the first faculty member hired at the college? Because the names were presented to the board alphabetically and because they had to vote on each recommendation separately, the first one voted on had to be Gerry Enscoe.

KT

Jericho's Walls

I have written here before about the modularity of the original buildings, about the ephemeral nature of our space and the fact that architectural design followed pedagogical function. To the Founders, these were unusual ideas in 1970, but we quickly saw their utility in our daily lives. Unfortunately, later buildings have rejected these concepts and we have moved backwards to designated and fixed pedagogical space.

I bring all of this up because I recently came across a *Press* article that describes "Planning Guidelines" in a document presented to the board of trustees sometime in 1970. So, I sent Louise Tillstrom in the college archives off on a search and she, of course, turned up the actual document in a trice.

That document is part of a "working paper" of the Campus Planning Committee which described concepts which any building should be designed around. The copy I have is dated June 1970. No author is noted though I suspect it was written by the Campus Planner—Dick Schwartz—for the committee.

The complete document is over 21 pages long and it describes a long list of facilities that were being planned: classroom space, laboratory/studio space, computer center services among them. The document comments on Phase I buildings—the very first buildings on campus (Wings A, B, C and D) with a student population in 1971 of 1000 students. It also comments on yet-to-be-built Phase II buildings completed in the Summer of 1972, with a student population of 2000 students.

Central to these concerns about new buildings and the students who would occupy them is the following statement:

> Preservation of the natural environment should continue to be a central objective.

Much has been said about this centrality of the environment from the very beginning of the college to the present; indeed there are several important essays in the book describing this centrality in the contexts of the Environmental Studies Program, its faculty and students, the history of the college situated in South Jersey, the rise of "sustainability" and the present emphasis on a "green college."

I will list a few of the other important considerations and then comment on their history.

> Faculty office areas are to be arranged in such a way that maximum exposure and intermixing of personnel from all academic disciplines will be encouraged. Isolation of any academic unit is to be avoided or other tendencies toward space "empire building."
> .....

> Often, colleges have been departmentalized or remain that way because specific buildings have been provided for specific units and their specialized functions. It is Stockton State's intent to promote greater interaction and integration among all programs, staff and students. This means the entire 7,500-student campus should be viewed as a "living-learning" center with as much mixing of academic, non-academic, living, etc. spaces as intelligent concern for logistics, traffic patterns, and workability permits. Perhaps

encouraging different people to come together more frequently takes precedence over the convenience and comfort of like-minded people being housed together.
.....

All administrative areas are to be readily accessible to faculty, students, staff and public. A separate administrative building should not be built and administrative spaces are to be located throughout all buildings with convenience to the user of the administrative function representing a more important consideration than convenience to the administrator.
.....

Traffic patterns should be designed to promote contact between commuter and residence students and this should be complemented by numerous small, informal spaces for people to stop and chat upon meeting.
.....

All spaces are to be planned with maximum flexibility so that areas can be used for more than one purpose. For example, science areas and art studios should be usable as classrooms with a furniture change.
.....

Exterior spaces are to be developed for use as seating, study, circulation, and communication areas with walks, benches, kiosks, attractive lighting, informal group seating, and even a few hideways.
.....

I suspect that most faculty today would find these "quaint" and terribly impractical. "Space that can be changed by changing the furniture?" "But what about the fact that I have just arranged the seats in a circle?" Or, "I can't teach in a classroom that doesn't have a podium."

Indeed, there has recently been a discussion about the arrangement of faculty offices. Younger faculty, who seem not to value living next to faculty not in their discipline, see no reason why offices should not cluster around a divisional center and, I might add, close to the copy machine and mail boxes. Older faculty seem to understand our original planning and seem to value living next door to humanists, mathematicians, chemists, accountants and nurses. If I had to bet on the outcome, I'd bet clustered offices will win and we will have lost another way of finding commonalities in our differences.

The present layout does work. I noticed today going to my class that at one end of the Gallery—where there are comfortable chairs overlooking the Arts and Sciences building—there were a dozen students chatting and typing on their computers.

As I walked down the stairs, I came upon an area of high tables near one of our coffee-snack bars. There were probably 30 or 40 students eating and drinking coffee in transit to or from a class.

In the same area, students were streaming in from parking lots and housing on the other side of the lake, who would peel-off to go upstairs to a class or further down the Gallery to another wing. Because this is in the oldest part of the complex, students have been doing these very things for 40 years. The spine of the campus is a street and it works wondrously. For me, we need more activity on this street. We need sales, art, drama—last year a medieval play was presented in the Gallery in front of the Library—announcements, foreign foods, demonstrations, quick classes, music.

The street could support the early conviction that the whole college be a living-learning center. Unfortunately, the lines separating spaces have been drawn though not as clearly as they are on many campuses. There are activities—musical events, comics and other performers—that are done in the dorm areas that do not appear on the street.

And what about meetings? While some areas of the Gallery are too raucous, there are places where, say, Student Senate meetings could be held. These are always held in some other, more interior space. Yet wouldn't it be exciting to see college democracy in action on the street?

We have managed to keep from building an administrative center though the presidential complex in one wing is close to it. Like the faculty, I suspect administrators would argue efficiency but that word can hide all sorts of not-particularly-efficient-activity.

Participatory democracy, decentralization, personalization, stressing commonalities, rejection of class, distrusting privilege and equality—all *de rigueur* in the 1960s and 1970s—seem old fashioned now. We took these very seriously on every level of our lives. It doesn't take much to hear these ideas in the Planning Guidelines above. We "operationalized" each and every one of them.

Finally, I come to "hideways." This is one idea that never appeared on campus and we are less for it. Why didn't small areas appear where both students and faculty could meet in some privacy? Was it because later planners distrusted students and faculty. Was it because it was not appropriate for the college to supply intimate space? I'm not sure; what I am sure of is that in a community of 8000 students and 300+ faculty, there are very few spaces that are even partially private. Humans, in my opinion, need such spaces—for rumination, meditation or simply to be alone for a few minutes before a class. All of this is moot, of course; no public institution today would risk public condemnation of such an idea. It is evident from the article where this discussion started; it ends with this statement:

> "Hideways?"
> "Yes, hideways. And that, students, is real togetherness!"

Our loss.

KT

The Dark Backward and Abysm Of Time

Rob and I have been looking through books of negatives to find photos we might use in the book. If a book contained a hundred negatives, it would be easy to create categories—sports, student life, classrooms, environment—assign the pictures to those categories and make a selection.

But we are looking at thousands! And they are not exactly what we want. Somewhere around a dozen or more large, green three-ring binders live in our graphics department cabinets. For each plastic sleeve of 35mm negative strips there is a contact sheet. And there are dozens and dozens of these sleeves and sheets in each volume.

Unfortunately for us, the dates on the green binders start at 1977—six years after the opening of the college.

This six year gap brings up some fascinating issues. Why don't we have pictures from the opening days?

A superficial excuse is because there was no specific photographer assigned to take "official" pictures. That assignment wasn't made until 1977.

A more helpful excuse has to do with the way we take photos now and the way we took them in 1970. Now, of course, you point and shoot and cameras are ubiquitous. In 1970 if I wanted to take a picture, I had to find my camera, had to make sure it had a roll of film in it and if not, had to go to a store to purchase it. Next I would have to install the film—all of this just to get ready to take a picture. Oh, yes, if it was dark, I had to find and take my flash attachment after making sure I had flashbulbs (repeat going to the store if I was out of bulbs).

I take the picture.

If color, I had to wait until all thirty-six shots had been taken, remove the role, place in a tiny can (assuming I could find it), insert the can into a tiny, yellow sack with a label attached. Then, fill out the label, add postage or get it at the Post Office and send it.

Then wait at least a week to get your slides returned.

If B&W film, I would remove the film, take it to a drug store or place where they would send the film off, it would be put in an envelope for pick-up, and wait for three days until the prints were returned to the store where I would pick them up.

Is it any wonder that photos were not shot and, hence, are not now available to us of events in 1970?

Also, I don't think that we thought that what we were doing was particularly photogenic, interesting or worthy of note. We met day after day to build a college. In hindsight, it was terribly important, but once started, as I remember it, it wasn't all that significant.

Photos were, of course, taken. I have the first *Prospectus* (1970) and the *Prospectus* from 1971. They both have "professional" looking photos. Not one of them notes the photographer or date. I have not turned them up in any of the collections at the college so far. The negatives seemed to have been shot by a staff member, printed and, probably, then discarded.

The few of these that we have are halftone pictures which do not have the high quality that we want in the book. Yet, they are all we have.

So, we need to find original negatives—if possible—and that means hours looking through green, three-ringed binders.

This looking is somewhat troublesome, at least to me. First of all, there is no classification system. They are not organized by subject, date or place. Volumes are labeled by year but within that category, who knows how they were organized. How easy it would have been to have used the spaces at the top of each page of sleeves—Date, Assignment, Number—but these were seldom filled in. Organizing by subject would be immensely helpful now. I could have looked for pictures of faculty, athletics, buildings, the environment, Lake Fred, the Courts or any of the many features of the college.

But this didn't occur. Now, each contact sheet has to be visually scanned (a loupe is essential) and when a desired photo is found, its page number must be written down (after carefully confirming that a negative for the photo exists in the sleeve) or confusion is added to confusion.

There is a "visual" thing going on as well. After about ten minutes looking at 35mm contact sheets, visual overload sets in. It's as if a very long film has been cut into individual frames, randomly mixed and then edited into a linear form. There simply is no linearity in this process or, more precisely, no linearity for more than a very few frames.

All of this confusion has an impact on judgment. If I have even five 35mm negatives in a row—say, shots of a basketball game. You know the scene: lithe bodies levitating towards the basket while a forest of arms struggle to stop the motion. You can hear the camera shouting click....buzz.... click....buzz....click...buzz...click; all motion captured but slightly different in each shot. Frames of a movie.

As I said, I can look at each frame making judgments about clarity, framing, are heads cut off, sharpness, etc. Knowing what I am looking for, I can make a judgment that frame four is exactly what I want.

But my judgment is impaired when I find two shots of the basketball game followed by a shot of six coeds walking through the halls to class followed by a shot of steel beams of a new building followed by a shot of two students in a canoe on Lake Fred. If I judge that one of these shots is good, exactly what I need, then fine. But if I have one or two of some person or activity, the narrative—to me, at least—seems gone. There is no encompassing context.

Now multiply this by forty-seven pages of sleeves each with thirty-five photos on each page. It isn't that the task is daunting—if not overwhelming. It's that after ten minutes it is impossible to do.

Then, of course, none of the persons in these shots are identified. Identification is a central issue in history books, I have found out. Rob and I want to be able to show a picture of faculty from forty years ago and have clear identification of each. Much of the time I can identify who they are—after all I was there—but others cannot provide identities and, therefore, such pictures simply become labeled "Faculty Members." Tragically, their narratives have been erased though their faces remain. It's like going through boxes of old photographs without knowing the identity of any.

History, then, has been subverted and, as a result, of minimal value. Ken Burns' genius is clear when he shows us a picture of what seems to be a nameless civil war soldier but then he adds the text of a letter and a name. We can connect that story with those eyes and history lives before us.

But what if you can't do that?

We have worked very hard to provide both the picture but, also, the life of the narrative of that picture. Much of the time we have succeeded; some of the time we have failed. But that's history too.

KT

How Does It Feel To Be Famous?

If the question "what was the most infamous incident in the early years of the College?" is asked to older faculty they will, without much hesitation, respond with two names: (1) the Candace Falk trial and (2) the Barense nude teaching class. The former seemed important then—Falk had asked Army recruiters to leave the campus; it was a very mild act of civil disobedience. They complied and Falk was later charged and brought before the Campus Hearing Board where she was acquitted. It was an early rejection of the Vietnam War and became a legend almost immediately.

The Barense case was, and is, far more serious and no less legendary. The popular myth has been that Jack Barense held a session of a class he was teaching at his home—in the nude. Though student disrobing was voluntary, as was that particular class, and though it was held at Barense's home, he was not, subsequently, retained. It would seem to be a classic violation of his academic freedom and that is the way it has been perceived for 40 years.

Recently, I was asked to write a short statement about academic freedom at Stockton and in thinking about the issue, I began to gather facts about Barense and the case. It is time, I submit, that those facts be reviewed and made public. There is no hidden scandal or villain in this case (exactly) but there are issues that in a different time would be critical to understand.

The Environment

It is necessary to examine the environment of the early College. When the College opened in 1971 there were no casinos and Atlantic City—once THE playground of the eastern part of the US—had fallen on very bad times. The largest employer was the FAA Tech Center (NAFEC). The urban blight of Atlantic City had spread throughout the eastern part of the county. Everything about the area was unattractive and unproductive.

There was also considerable distrust of the College. The public seemed torn between pleasure at having a major institution of higher education dropped in its lap and genuine distrust about what its intentions were. Carl McIntyre's protest of the College claiming that it supported and taught revolutionary communism was real, though slightly ridiculous. While his congregation was tiny, his views were certainly shared by many in the area.

Once the College had moved to the present campus in 1972, there seemed to be constant offenses to the popular culture. There was bra burning at the quintessential American event—the Miss America Pageant. There were class trips to cut sugar cane in Communist Nicaragua and to DC to protest the Vietnam War. There were two incidents that must have also concerned the local community: a photographer took pictures of nude sunbathing at Lake Pam and of the "clothing optional" sauna below the I-Wing gym.

South Jersey was conservative, religious, insulated, rural and undeveloped. It was into this environment that Jack Barense stepped when he took a teaching job here in 1972.

Why Barense Was Hired In the Management Sciences Division

Wes Tilley—the first VP of Academic Affairs—did not like business schools and the courses they offered. In Tilley's view, they were anti-liberal arts and anti-humanities and that was sufficient for him to distrust them.

This is one of the reasons why the Management Sciences dean was not hired when the other deans were (summer 1970); indeed, that dean was hired in January of 1971—well after the work, the collaboration and a resultant community was well founded by the other four deans.

Further, Tilley specifically looked for candidates who had a strong background in the humanities and strong intentions to mold business majors into broadly educated graduates.

One decision—and this is the very root of this whole issue—was to insist on hiring a philosopher to teach in the management programs. Tilley's argument was that such a teacher could teach ethics, logic, decision-making and leadership but from a philosophical perspective. As it happened, Barense was that philosopher.

In hindsight, it would have been incredibly better to have hired Barense in the Philosophy Program and then to have asked him to teach courses for management and business.

But that wasn't what was done. The fact that there was a philosopher in the Management Sciences division becomes part of the argument which was used against Barense a year or so after his arrival. More on this later.

The Basic Facts

It is important, at this point, to understand the fundamental facts of what happened. In the spring of 1974, Jack Barense taught two sections of a General Studies course— GS 3240 Workshop in Sexism. This course was, essentially, a re-designed course he had previously taught—GS 3321 Sexism as a Social Problem. It is unclear whether his wife, Diane, co-taught the course, participated in the design of the course, was paid for her efforts or what, exactly, her role was.

Barense described the focus of both courses in a statement to Robert Helsabeck dated July 26, 1974. Sexism as a Social Problem "was traditionally academic in that the focus was on various sociological, political, psychological, and anthropological studies of sexism." The subsequent course—Workshop In Sexism—"was designed to focus on those elements of sexism as a social problem which seemed to most strongly motivate most of the participants to think critically about sexism; namely, personal examinations of sexism in their own lives."

These classes had recommended readings, though "academic materials were only used for background reference, seldom as the focus of discussion. It was clear that much reading was done by some participants, little by others." Nowhere that I could find in the documents is there any mention of tests or papers.

Sequence of Courses

Spring 1973   GS 3321 - Sexism As A Social Problem
Fall 1973   GS 3321 - Sexism As A Social Problem
Spring 1974   GS 3240 - Workshop On Sexism
Fall 1974   GS 3240 - Workshop On Sexism

Nudity

It needs to be clear that Barense had had nude sessions in each of these courses. He mentions in a memo to John

Rickert, Dean of Management Sciences (October 31, 1974), that his class had visited a local nudist camp in the Spring of 1973. Fourteen members of that class disrobed. He does not mention whether or not nude sessions were held in the Fall 1973 class; given his commitment to the technique one can easily assume they were.

There were two sections of the class in the Spring of 1974 and in both nudity was employed. Indeed, in one section, a student's mother participated but the daughter didn't. This group did not again disrobe because "the good feelings of the nude participants were, they reported, spoiled by the non-participants." The other section was so pleased by the experience that they met a number of times in the nude.

As I have mentioned, there were two contemporary incidents of nudity at Stockton; they were photos taken at Lake Pam (Lake Pam is a small pond on campus with a "nude" beach) and in the sauna under the gym.

While certainly not a national movement, there were frequent episodes of public nudity in the late 1960s to early 1970s. There were streakers at major athletic or musical events; there was considerable nudity at Woodstock in 1969 and there was some nudity in college drama.

The Unofficial Story

Barense maintained, after the start of the grievance process, that there were two versions of the administration's narrative: the official version and the unofficial version.

Barense, in a memo to the College Review Board dated December 1, 1974, claimed that the incident began on October 31, 1974, when he was pulled from his class to meet with John Rickert. At that meeting, Rickert reported that "Vice President Thrombley was furious over reports that I had used nude exercises. . ." and that "he was taking a lot of heat on this one." Barense's response was that he would write an explanation for Rickert but the dean responded by predicting "that it would not mollify Woody."

There is an interesting time shift in all of this. First the class with the nude session that had triggered the administrative response was held in the Spring of 1974—some six months before the talk with Rickert in October. Also, Robert Helsabeck's request for information about the course came in late July of 1974—some three months before the talk with Rickert. It is difficult not to conclude that the administration knew about the nude sessions but had done nothing about them until October. It's possible that Thrombley had not been pressured by someone off campus until October when he "took a lot of heat." I believe that it is outside pressure that began the process of rejecting Barense. Had only a few on campus known about the nudity—as it seems they did all through the Spring and Summer of 1974—not much would have happened. But pressure from the outside couldn't be ignored, so Thrombley moved aggressively to demand it stop.

Once Thrombley had ordered Rickert to direct Barense to cease the nude sessions and to move the class back on campus—Barense ultimately agreed to this demand—in a memo from Rickert to Barense dated November 1, 1974, it seemed that the issue was settled.

Barense signaled his compliance to Thrombley's demands in a letter dated November 15, 1974, and, there, he also announced his intention to begin grievance procedures.

The Official Story

With the filing of the grievance, the problem becomes one for the administration. Barense claimed that in a meeting with Thrombley on November 7, 1974, the latter admitted that a small, intimate class might be better in a home and that Thrombley was willing to allow meetings there but that Barense could not use nude exercises. Yet in a memo from Thrombley dated November 11, 1974, Thrombley ordered Barense to conduct the class on campus and not to use nude exercises.

At this point, the evaluation process had begun and on November 6, 1974, the Faculty Review Committee voted eight to one to recommend reappointment. On November 13, 1974, John Rickert's recommendations were sent to Thrombley but they were returned to Rickert a couple of days later "for corrections." Rickert's first evaluation was positive, recommending Barense for reappointment. By November 20, 1974, Rickert recommended that Barense *not* be reappointed.

Thrombley submitted his recommendations to President Bjork on November 20, 1974, as well as including the recommendation that Barense not be reappointed.

Rickert's Claim

In late June and early July 1975 at an arbitration hearing, Barense, under oath, gave the following as testimony:

> I was very surprised when Dean Rickert said that he had not himself recommended me for retention. He said that he had intended to do so; that he very much wanted to do so but that Vice-President Thrombley had told him that if he did this he would reverse him; that the Vice-President would reverse Dean Rickert, and in addition would put some dirty information into my file. Dean Rickert said that he himself felt that he could put a negative recommendation into my file which would give just institutional reasons and be able then to give me a very positive recommendation for a position elsewhere, and he

thought he was doing me a favor by submitting to the pressure from the Vice President.

He said, however, he didn't even—well, he said that his original recommendation which had very little negative information into which it just gave institutional priorities of need for accountants over people with my schooling. He said that that memo which was sent back to him—that original recommendation was sent back to him on the 15th and he said not by accident on the 15th, that being the day that I filed my grievance together with an angry memo, handwritten memo, from the Vice President—"Look, you got to get more negative stuff on Barense. This isn't strong enough and if you don't I'm still going to put in a negative information myself into his file." So, the Dean said he then wrote a second letter of recommendation, not making it clear whether he had taken the first one out or whether the Vice President had taken the first one out, and in this he said, 'Well, I really couldn't come up with any additional negative information of any substance....' Dean Rickert said that he probably made a mistake in submitting to the pressures of the Vice President; that I probably would have a strong case with a grievance filed, but that he said I was indeed a very clever fellow. I could probably find in the record enough information to undo whatever harm he had done me in this respect. ... He did say that, of course, the whole thing was a result of having filed the grievance of the Workshop having used the nude exercises and of having filed a grievance trying to protect my right to use those in the future. He also did say that he would deny everything that he was telling me outside that room.

If true, this is an astounding report. First of all, it is a violation of the AFT Agreement where Article VI, Section I states that "no reprisal of any kind shall be taken against any participant in this grievance procedure by reason of proper participation in such procedure." It seems clear today that, again, if the Rickert remarks are true, Thrombley's anger resulting from Barense's grievance is being used against Barense's reappointment. Indeed, John Searight, Chairman of the SFT Grievance Committee, says this in a letter to President Bjork dated December 16, 1974.

In addition, Searight states that in spite of the requirement that all documents put into a faculty evaluation file have to be copied to the faculty member, neither the first positive recommendation nor the second negative recommendation were sent to Barense.

Saying that not retaining Barense is really helping him sounds like something a person might concoct when caught between a rock and a hard place.

Finally, Thrombley's insistence that Rickert must find "more negative stuff" speaks volumes about Thrombley's anger and desire to be rid of Barense.

The Telephone Call

Rickert states in the second, negative recommendation—dated November 18, 1974—that he had spoken with Barense's dissertation director at the University of Wisconsin to ascertain what progress Barense was making, if any, towards completing his dissertation and earning a Ph.D. It is certainly acceptable for a Dean to put pressure on a faculty to complete a degree. The curious issue here, however, is that there is *no* requirement that a faculty have a Ph.D. to be retained. A faculty only needs a higher degree to be granted tenure which, of course, Barense was not seeking.

Further, this seems like the kind of "negative stuff" that Thrombley asked Rickert to find. The "negative stuff" is—first paragraph—that "In a period of scarce resources, we cannot afford to continue to hold a position that does not maximize the needs in course work for the Management Sciences Division." In the second paragraph, Barense is not to be retained because he hasn't finished his degree. In the fifth paragraph, Barense is unsatisfactory because he hasn't given promised guest lectures. Finally, in the sixth paragraph, Barense did not "follow through with these suggestions (some sort of suggestions made before a Faculty Review meeting) or even his own suggestions."

Rickert claims in this same letter that "earlier in the month [November] he had placed a call to Barense's dissertation director. But going through College phone records, Barense found that the call had been made on November 20, 1974, two days *after* the recommendation not to retain had been written and placed in Barense's file!

It seems clear, though it is impossible to prove with documents, that Rickert first wrote a positive letter. Under intense pressure from Thrombley, he was forced to secretly retract that letter and write another filled with "negative stuff."

When asked, under oath in July 1975, about the discrepancy between the dates of the telephone call Rickert "offered no explanation (and no satisfactory explanation on cross examination) for the patently false statement, 'according to a conversation . . . earlier this month'."

The Missing Document
John Rickert wrote his initial, positive recommendation on November 13, 1974, but Thrombley had returned it to him "along with several other documents . . . being not in good form and frankly rather sloppy." When asked by the Arbitrator

in July 1975, Rickert replied that "Those documents are still in existence for all the different people [faculty]. There were a few, you know, kept on each person."

The importance of this November 13th recommendation cannot be overstated. Having it would show precisely what Rickert's initial evaluation of Barense had been and compared to the later negative recommendation would have implicated both Rickert and Thrombley in a conspiracy to change a document supposed to have been kept secure in the file.

Thus the Arbitrator agreed to allow a search for the documents during one lunch recess. After the recess, the testimony records the exchange between the Arbitrator and Dean Rickert:

> Arbitrator: . . . Dr. Rickert informed us that the document which was to be produced at the end of the recess was, in his mind, the final recommendation by him and not as was intended by the Arbitrator the November 13th recommendation, and that the November 13th recommendation is no longer in existence.

Not only had the document been destroyed but, though Rickert initially claimed that he was thinking of the November 13th version, after the recess he claimed that the version he meant as still existing was the November 18th version and that the earlier version has been destroyed.

There was, therefore, no means of proving that the original document had existed—except for Barense's claim—and that it had been changed from positive to negative most likely under Thrombley's direction.

Penultimate Comments

Throughout the grievance process—the Agreement lists four distinct steps—the whole issue of academic freedom had been lost in favor of more provable claims that the process of reappointment had been violated. For six months the claims and counter-claims droned on. At each stage of the grievance process, the final decisions made by President Bjork were negative: Barense was not to be reappointed.

Indeed, that final decision could only be made by Bjork, unless the whole struggle ended in the courts. Even the final Arbitrator's July 1975 opinion could only recommend an ad hoc committee to re-examine the long, sad struggle.

But Jack Barense had moved on. For a time he worked with the ACLU in New Jersey and then went to law school earning a JD so he could practice public defender law. Sadly, Jack Barense died in 2002.

I am not aware that he ever taught again.

What about Academic Freedom?

If we lived in a dictatorship or in a society of robots, we would have little need for statements about academic freedom. In such a society, each of us would teach what we were told to teach. In such societies, literature tells us, there is always some individual, some single entity who refuses the directions and demands of the group. This is true in *1984* and in *I, Robot*.

There are, therefore, two parts to any concept of academic freedom. The first has to do with the degree of restrictions laid on the individual by the group. The second has to do with the individual and how she responds to the directions of that group. Thus, the 1940 statement of the AAUP addresses itself to both parties. In that statement, the demand that the group offer and support academic freedom for the individual is clearly stated. But, also clearly stated, is the responsibility of the individual in expressing that academic freedom.

The fundamental, underlying principle in any discussion of academic freedom—and this is where all discussions must start—must be, as the 1940 statement makes clear, that "the common good depends upon the free search for truth and its free exposition." If all parties do not agree with this fundamental principle then any discussion of academic freedom will be nearly impossible to undertake.

In an already established college, the dimensions and qualities of the "free search for truth" are well-known, have been thoroughly tested and are part of the institutional culture. Thus, if I had been hired as a new faculty in an established college, I would have been given already written syllabi with established texts and assignments to teach. After a few years of obedient service, I would have been allowed, perhaps, to select my preferred texts and to make my designed assignments. Eventually as I rose through the ranks, I would have been allowed to design whole courses as long as they fit into departmental curricula.

Stockton, however, was in the unique position of having the new faculty design and implement the curricula considered, by them, to be appropriate and relevant to themselves and to their students. In a very real way, they designed the institution in which they were going to teach. They became both the group and the individuals in that group.

In 1970, both the administration and the faculty understood that the faculty brought with them appropriate professional goals and that those goals would be realized in individual, program curricula. For example, the founding Dean of Arts and Humanities assumed that his literature faculty knew how to construct a curriculum appropriate to the field of literature and one which could stand the scrutiny of other departments of literature in other colleges. In other words, he felt assured that his faculty knew what the "free search for truth" meant for teachers of literature and that they would produce a curriculum that would manifest that search.

This assumption was true across the college and across all disciplines. We all understood that the faculty would create programs of learning that were like most other programs of learning in other institutions.

My point in this is to assert that the "free search for truth" was well understood, well implemented and defensible at Stockton in 1970. There was no need—nor was there any intention—for the administration to create curricula before the faculty had input. So, the possibility of limiting the faculty's "free search for truth" was never considered. We wanted, and trusted, the faculty to create their own curricula.

It was in the area of "free exposition" that problems occurred. There is no doubt that history had "set us up for conflict." First of all, was the revolution of the 1960s going on in America, which by 1970 had spilled over into academia. In addition, Stockton hired the youngest faculty in the state. These young men and women were increasingly resistant to older, restrictive power arrangements. Also, we had presented the new college as being genuinely new. Faculty were attracted to Stockton solely for that reason. Finally, old definitions of what teaching was and the style in which it was done were being roundly rejected.

It was certainly clear to the founding administration that the rules of power, the content of the curricula and the relationships between faculty and students were going to be tested.

It didn't help that we opened in a derelict hotel in Atlantic City. There was very little about us that looked like, sounded like or felt like a traditional college. Given all of this, one might expect that Stockton was a hotbed of controversy over academic freedom. One might expect that a restrictive administration would be constantly in conflict with the permissive faculty teaching radical social, political, cultural ideas to unsuspecting, first-generation college students. If one assumed that he would be wrong. Most courses and most teachers taught traditional material in generally traditional ways.

I've included this sad case at this point because it seems, in hindsight, to be a classic incident of the threat to academic freedom. The teacher was free to design the course as he saw fit. The administration seems to have seen the incident as an example of bad judgment, threatening the wider reputation of the college in the community and against the values and mores of the larger society.

Indeed, the college had been featured in the local press as supportive of a nudist beach at Lake Pam and a clothes-optional sauna in the gym. The wider community had condemned the college for these incidents so the college was especially sensitive to the nude encounter.

In spite of the fact that the panel did not conclude that academic freedom had been violated, it does seem to be a classic confrontation. The teacher designed the course to include various learning experiences. The administration saw the incident as beyond the pale of acceptable pedagogy and, therefore, a threat to the whole institution.

Stockton has been fortunate (this is, I suggest, due to its newness) in not having many confrontations over academic freedom. There is a long history now of faculty determining what is pedagogically appropriate and of designing courses that include those experiences. But, and understanding this is critical, there are lines which, if crossed, may well produce a confrontation. Once again, all of this supports the principles stated in the 1940 statement.

I believe that the insistence of the 1940 statement that there be a balance between an individual's opinion and the wider, traditional search for the truth is vital and critically necessary for democracy to exist. We must be permitted to express our beliefs but we also must be prepared to accept the consequences of that expression. That balance is absolutely essential in an institution of higher learning.

KT

One of These Things Is
Not Like The Others

It is not much of an overstatement to say that I spent twenty-five percent of my time as the Founding Dean of General Studies trying to explain what a General Studies course was and how it was different, say, from an introductory course in a traditional discipline.

I interviewed every candidate we brought to the campus including those we didn't hire. This was my primary chance to explain what I had in mind about General Studies and how they would participate in that curriculum. I also inquired about courses that they wanted to teach but, for a variety of reasons, had not done so. Not wanting to seem too radical, most suggested courses in their disciplines but for a general audience. Having gotten that out of the way, I then asked about what courses outside of their field they felt qualified to teach.

At this point they usually tried to escape my probing by saying that they hadn't given such courses much thought. This response usually caused me to question whether they should be hired.

Those who had thought about such courses responded eagerly giving me four or five examples of courses they "had always wanted to teach." These were the excited—and exciting—candidates who got a strong, positive response from me.

This was, of course, only one of the criteria that I used to make judgments about candidates. Some of the ones who

213

hadn't thought about such courses responded when I made suggestions. Some of those who had such courses in mind faded when I asked questions about resources they would need, about assignments, about how the course might be structured and about what sorts of students they imagined taking the course.

Interviewing for a non-existent college was complex, lengthy, sometimes contentious, always probing and I absolutely assumed that if a candidate had been invited to the campus she was worthy of my respect and support.

Keep in mind that candidates coming to the campus had already been showered with our position papers, Academic Working Papers and any other writings we had produced. We did this, of course, so they wouldn't be under any false expectations about what we were, what we expected of them and what they could expect from us.

One of my favorite approaches was the "Year" course. If candidates were stumped about what to teach as a General Studies course, I would suggest that they think of a year significant in their field or to them and design a course around that year as a theme. This comes from a very old desire on my part to teach a course called "1381." For England, this is a critical year. For example, it is the year of the Peasant's Revolt so there are economic and political issues that could be investigated. It is also a significant year for architecture in that Richard II rebuilt Westminster Hall, supported all of the arts which environment, in turn, gave Geoffrey Chaucer opportunities to write his later works. Two issues about which historians have argued since the nineteenth century are Richard's concept of kingship and his fragile mental state.

Under the theme of a single year, then, my course in 1381 might contain political, historical, artistic, literary and psychological issues. Such a course could be designed on almost any year.

It would be a suitable General Studies course because it would be interdisciplinary, unlike most courses in the disciplines, precisely focused, introductory and would permit the faculty member to teach a bit outside of her comfort zone.

The Definitions of a General Studies Course

So the simplest definition is that a General Studies course is interdisciplinary, not a traditional introduction, can be outside of the instructor's disciplinary training, can be current and involves risk on both the faculty's and student's part.

Saying this does not make creating such a course easy, however.

Imagine that I am a young medievalist just hired by Stockton to teach medieval literature. I have taught—or would know how to design and teach—the following medieval courses:

1. A survey of medieval literature
2. A course in the writings of Chaucer
3. A course on Beowulf and Old English
4. A course on medieval romance
5. A course on minor works of the Middle Ages

This is wonderful for the Literature Program; these courses are exactly what I was hired to teach.

What, however, can I teach in General Studies? I can't simply teach an introduction to Chaucer or Beowulf using translations. The minor works are too specialized for a general audience. I might be able to design a course using medieval romances in translation especially if I organized it thematically. But I am still limited by concepts of discipline, my graduate experience and what's appropriate for literature majors.

Students in a General Studies class will not all be literature majors; as a matter of fact, frequently few of them are. This means that they have little experience with the conceptual basis of literature—genres, symbols, criticisms, characterization, plot structure, etc.—so the instructor cannot assume they do. Another way of looking at the type of student is to understand that a General Studies course—unlike a course for literature majors—is not open-ended.

When I teach literature majors I assume that they have had some exposure to this conceptual basis and that they will have more and different exposure to it in the literature courses of my colleagues. General Studies students, on the other hand, may only take my General Studies course and never again take another literature course. If I am going to prepare them to read literature carefully and sensitively, I have to do it in this one course.

I am not, of course, suggesting that a conceptual basis not be part of a General Studies course. In some ways, it is an even more important part given that such information will be often repeated in a course for majors. For example, I always review the Five Act structure that Shakespeare used in all of his plays though I understand that some of my students will have covered it in other courses in the major. It is, in my opinion, a central issue in General Studies courses.

The idea of a set of concepts underlying and/or preceding the content of a course has become a problem over the forty years of General Studies. As the leadership and acculturation of what a General Studies course has declined, young faculty increasingly imported introductory courses from the major into their contributions to the General Studies curriculum. If I am a young, rising faculty member striving to get tenure and a promotion and believing that that tenure and promotion depends almost totally on the teaching I do for majors and the research I do in my discipline, what I do in General Studies seems vastly less important. Generating and teaching new courses is hard work so, many of these young faculty seem to conclude, why not teach a watered down version of what I teach to beginning majors? Unfortunately, General Studies teaching has not always been viewed as an important element in decisions about promotion and tenure.

How Is the General Studies Student Viewed?

When I was the Dean, I had clear ideas about how students taking General Studies courses should be viewed:

> 1. We did not need college-wide requirements for General Studies courses.
> 2. We did not see ourselves as "redeeming" the student.
> 3. We did not see ourselves and our work as the beginning of education.
> 4. The General Studies experience was not a foundation for the major.
> 5. General Studies courses were to be taken throughout the student's stay at the College.

College-Wide Requirements

Frankly, I have never seen a need for college-wide requirements in general education. What sorts of requirements specific disciplines create is their business. We all assume they know the field and can match requirements for majors to their field.

But general education need not be so restrictive.

Such requirements are the result of attitudes about students: "they are unformed clay and desperately need shaping by elders," "they are dolts who need 'redeeming' from their doltish state" and "they are at the beginning of education

and, thus, need introductions to as many of the traditional disciplines as can be crammed into the first two years."...
I reject and rejected forty years ago all of these assumptions.

Students came to Stockton forty years ago—and today as well—having all sorts of preferences and opinions about their futures. These were not and are not always correct but they had information about what they wanted to do.

What they needed—as we viewed students forty years ago—was to be challenged with other information, other opinions and facts. That was the fundamental role of the preceptor as we originally conceived of that person.

There is, admittedly, a thin line between requiring and advising. To require means that all students have the same needs and that, left to their own devices, would continue in their ignorant bliss. Requirements also assume that all students need, say, a biology or math course and that all students learn the same way.

Advising personalizes and tailors the curriculum to the student's past and future ("I never like studying a language but I want to be a public school teacher in New Jersey"). It is based on face to face contact and not some list of required courses on a sheet of paper.

Introductions

I also rejected the assumption that beginning students needed introductions. All courses are "introductions" to students. In one sense, all General Studies courses are introductions for the students. They were not and should not be today deliberately designed as introductions.

The course in "1381" that I described above will certainly be an introduction. Almost all students don't know a single fact about that year. But my design of the course would be radically different from a traditional Introduction to

218

the Middle Ages. First of all, such an introduction would include works from Anglo-Saxon texts through Malory in the fourteenth century. The course in 1381 would, per force, only include works from that year. Such an introduction would include the major genres of literature; my course would probably not include them. An introduction would probably offer texts in translation; mine would be read in the original Middle-English. An introduction might not offer contextual/ancillary readings at all; mine would be full of them. An introduction might not include definitions of terms; mine would be filled with such definitions.

Faculty, generally, would prefer to teach traditional introductions in General Studies because that is the easiest route. I rejected this desire and urged/forced faculty to teach new courses that were not easy or cut-and-dried. From the beginning, I saw the General Studies curriculum as a powerful way for faculty to grow; as powerful as it was for students.

Taken Each Term for Four Years

Because I rejected these assumptions, it became clear that students should take General Studies courses throughout their four years at Stockton. If one conceives of general education as a foundation for all other disciplinary courses, then it makes sense to take up the first four terms with general education. After this probationary period students can go on to the major of their choice.

But, once all this traditional underbrush is cut away, it becomes clear that they should take General Studies course throughout their work at Stockton.

To conclude, then, a General Studies course at Stockton should fit the following criteria:

1. It is not an "introduction" brought into General Studies from a disciplinary major.
2. It is a fabulous opportunity for faculty to try new courses, new pedagogical techniques and new approaches to old material.
3. It is a "closed experience" in that faculty must not assume students will build on a single course.
4. It is a course that includes all sorts of contextual content.
5. It is not a course that will lead to specialized knowledge, a job or eternal happiness. It is its own justification.
6. Good General Studies courses show relationships, continuities, connections. Other courses *may* do these things but General Studies courses do them deliberately.
7. A General Studies course makes few assumptions about the students in the course.
8. A General Studies course is a time for both faculty and student to "try" something.

I can't say that, on the many, many occasions when I was asked to define a General Studies course, I was very successful. Over the months, however, I did develop what I felt then and feel now was a successful way of talking about these courses. I argued that the curriculum of a major would prepare a student for a career in that discipline. Thus, the Literature faculty would offer courses that would make it possible for students to teach literature in high school.

General Studies courses, I argued, were for all of the other "identities" we carry with us: the spouse, the lover, the citizen, the tax-payer, the consumer, the parent, etc. What part of the college experience educates those folks? That's the role of the General Studies curriculum.

I believed that forty years ago and I believe it even more intensely now.

KT

Epilogue

Reaching 40 in Beijing

I gave copies of *Reaching 40* to some faculty and administrators at the University of International Business and Economics in Beijing. This was a gift, but it was also part of an effort to help them understand what it is that Stockton is and what it is like. If they are to work with us and create articulations of any kind, then they should have a better sense of Stockton and I hoped that the book would be useful in this regard.

It turns out that I may have been correct in this. The following day after giving out the book, one of the professors informed me that she was very impressed with the volume and found it a particularly enjoyable read. What she felt most intrigued by was the fact that as a volume commemorating the history of the college it wasn't merely celebratory, which any volume about a Chinese university would have been. She was most impressed with this and found it inspiring, and she hoped that her colleagues would also. She herself believed in being critical and not merely accepting the positions of a regime, but she was surprised to see that a volume of this nature would also end up as an arena for critical analysis.

I indicated to her that this book was unusual for any commemorative volume in the United States as well, and that this is one of the things that makes Stockton unique—or distinctive, if you will—that it has always had spirited debate and conflict, and that it is for this reason that we (the editors) did not feel we should shy away from controversy in our anniversary volume.

RG

Blogging 40

Colophon

Taylor Cills and Diondra Meningall-Burney, editing interns at Stockton University during fall 2017, and Margaret Simek, editing intern during spring 2018, edited and designed this volume. Jena Brignola designed the cover. Tom Kinsella supervised the publication.

The text is set in 12 point Adobe Caslon Pro.

The mission of the South Jersey Culture & History Center is to help foster awareness within local communities of the rich cultural and historical heritage of southern New Jersey, to promote the study of this heritage, especially among area students, and to produce publishable materials that provide lasting and deepened understanding of this heritage.

CPSIA information can be obtained
at www.ICGtesting.com
Printed in the USA
BVHW070728200219
540696BV00001B/3/P